TILL THE NIGHT BE PAST

TILL THE NIGHT BE PAST

The Life and Times of Dietrich Bonhoeffer

THEODORE J. KLEINHANS

CPH.
SAINT LOUIS

Scripture quotations taken from the King James or Authorized Version of the Bible.

Copyright © 2002 Theodore J. Kleinhans
Published by Concordia Publishing House
3558 S. Jefferson Avenue, St. Louis, MO 63118-3968

Manufactured in the United States of America

Cover photograph of Dietrich Bonhoeffer copyright © Chr. Kaiser/Gütersloher Verlagshaus GmbH, Gütersloh.
Barbed wire photograph copyright © Nonstock/Robert Bergman-Ungar.

Library of Congress Cataloging-in-Publication Data

Kleinhans, Theodore J.
   Till the night be past : the life and times of Dietrich Bonhoeffer /
Theodore J. Kleinhans.
     p. cm.
   Includes bibliographical references.
   ISBN 0-570-05290-4
   1. Bonhoeffer, Dietrich, 1906–1945. 2. Theologians—Germany—Biography.
I. Title.
   BX4827.B57 K57 2002
   230'.044'092—dc21   2001006191

1 2 3 4 5 6 7 8 9 10   11 10 09 08 07 06 05 04 03 02

Contents

Foreword

The fascination with Dietrich Bonhoeffer continues in the 21st century. One cannot help admiring his persistence in the faith to the point of martyrdom. To some Christians today, he appears to be a Protestant saint, to others a modern theologian, his life's work, unfortunately, unfinished. The differing views may be the very problem in evaluating this German churchman, theological scholar, dedicated ecumenicist, instructor of opponent vicars, and, finally, anti-Nazi conspirator.

In his *Letters and Papers from Prison*, some nontraditional terms give the impression Bonhoeffer was on the verge of reconstructing Christian thought. Indeed, expressions such as *cheap grace, religionless Christianity, a world come of age, Christian worldliness*, or the idea that "Christians [should] participate in the suffering of God in the life of the world" may seem strange to the eyes of readers who are used to more traditional, particularly Lutheran, terminology.

There are many contradictions and tensions in Bonhoeffer's life and writings, but much continuity and significance. In prison, he once styled himself a "liberal" theologian. Indeed, he went through a process of theological development at the Berlin university under the guidance of one of the most famous liberal theologians in Germany, Reinhold Seeberg. Following that, Bonhoeffer became more acquainted with the *Book of Concord* of the Lutheran Church, particularly with the *Formula of Concord*. During his work as an instructor of vicars of the Confessing Church in the mid-1930s, he began weighing with a great deal of respect the solutions to the theological and ecclesiastical problems of the late Reformation era developed by the second-generation Lutheran theologians.

Bonhoeffer was ordained a pastor of the Old Prussian Church, a "united" church body of Lutherans and Reformed brought together at the beginning of the 19th century under the Prussian Union. However, Bonhoeffer criticized the proposals of the Halle synod of the Confessing Church as theologically immature because they advocated church fellowship with all its members, whether Lutheran, Reformed, or "united."

One of the crucial issues in Bonhoeffer's theological development was how to convey the Gospel message to modern, secular human beings. He was consumed by a desire to apply the Gospel to his world, to make it understandable and relevant for the men and women of his day. Traditional ways of expressing the faith appeared no longer helpful. *Religion* as he understood it—in a way similar to Karl Barth's view—was an old-fashioned, unsuitable form of piety, cut off from real life and the needs of the modern world. Given these presuppositions, traditional Christian language seemed to make God appear ineffective and makeshift (*Lückenbüßer*, "stop-gap"). In the modern worldview, God became important only at the borders of life, yet Bonhoeffer was deeply convinced that God belongs right in the center of human activity. Bonhoeffer was eager for Christianity to be *contemporary*. What he, therefore, proposed was an expression of the faith intelligible to post-Christian, secular humankind. In his thinking, this was merely the logical consequence of defining Jesus Christ as "a man for others"—a new Christological title invented by Bonhoeffer himself. Transferred into ecclesiastical language, this included the *church* of Christ becoming a "church for others." In this manner, he tried to explain common Christian terms such as *sacrifice* or *devotion*.

In the modern environment, as Bonhoeffer analyzed it, intellectuals, teachers, engineers, and lawyers were abandoning the church because it no longer answered the questions that disturbed them. They were incapable of understanding the traditional terms the church was using. Bonhoeffer contended the church, therefore, should not object to reformulating central Christian issues for modern seekers of religious truth. He believed the crisis was not the fault of his fellow citizens, but of the church and its leaders' inability to demonstrate the relevance of biblical truths. That forced modern intellectuals to abandon an obsolete and antiquated church.

One might conclude that Bonhoeffer underestimated the real meaning of *religion* (which should not to be confused with *faith*) as a part of the human condition. From one point of view, even the Nazi parades and the staging of their annual party meetings at Nuremberg were "religious," using a horrifying, worldly kind of liturgy. The popularity of Eastern religions (touted as post-Christian) and their influence on Western people today clearly demonstrate a similar strong yearning for something satisfying and *transcendental* shared even by secularized people of our day.

One might even question the suggestion by Bonhoeffer to reformulate Christian faith to gain a convincing contemporary witness to the Bible's truth. His attempts to solve the problems of Christian witness in post-Christian times remain controversial. Yet Bonhoeffer's life and writings are still important and ought to be thoroughly considered, unless we, too, want to lose contact with real people.

Bonhoeffer was certainly not a confessional Lutheran in the traditional sense of the term, but today he encourages us to focus anew on a convincing and satisfying witness of the Gospel. The least we can say is that he authenticated this quest and testified to it by his death.

One of the last statements from Bonhoeffer celebrates his faith:

> I am so sure of God's guiding hand that I hope I shall always be kept in that certainty. You must never doubt that I am traveling with gratitude and cheerfulness along the road where I am being led. My past life is brimful of God's goodness and my sins are covered by the forgiving love of Christ crucified. I am most thankful for the people I have met, and I only hope that they never have to grieve about me, but that they, too, will always be certain of, and thankful for, God's mercy and forgiveness.

May God give us this confidence and hope in our day.

—Dr. Werner Klän
Oberursel, Germany

Preface

I first became acquainted with Dietrich Bonhoeffer at Concordia Seminary, St. Louis, in 1950 through reading *The Cost of Discipleship* and *Letters and Papers from Prison*. Upon graduation, I went to work for Stewart Herman and Carl Lund-Quist at the Lutheran World Federation in Geneva. Because Bonhoeffer spent so much time on the common campus of the World Council of Churches and the Lutheran World Federation, he was at the time of my tenure, and still is today, regarded by many theologians as a courageous social activist and outspoken realist, a member of a rich family who was murdered for his opposition to the Nazis and to Hitler. There were some churchmen who did not think Bonhoeffer's decision to seek a military chaplaincy or later to become a secret operative for the Abwehr were wise.

Later, I came to know more about Bonhoeffer from a young lady I sailed with on the Wannsee in Berlin. She had heard his final sermon at the boarding school at Schoenberg in Bavaria, a location where both of them were interned during Bonhoeffer's final weeks of life. This young lady was a member of one of the high-ranking military families that, after the July 20 plot against Hitler, were interned, whether or not they had any connection with the plotters. As one prison after another was bombed, Bonhoeffer ended up by mistake at Schoenberg for a few weeks before being taken to Flossenbürg to be hanged in the last days of the war.

What is Bonhoeffer's role in Christianity today? Among some American theologians, he is revered as one whose concepts and theology, in his own words, had "come of age." Among European students of theology, Bonhoeffer is more apt to be thought of as a bold and courageous defender of the church who, as Ingetraut Ludophy once wrote, was not so much concerned about the "other-worldliness" of the church as for its "this-worldliness." They also reflect on his shortened life in which his theology did not have a full opportunity to develop and on his practical protest against the evil of his times.

I was involved to a small degree with shaping a film about Bonhoeffer for broadcast on public television in the summer of 2000. The film, *Dietrich Bonhoeffer: Agent of Grace,* showed some of the conflict in Dietrich's personality: his practical involvement with the world of politics and at the same time his eagerness not to give up the God whom he had come to understand and live with. From the reactions to the film in Germany and in America, it is evident that Bonhoeffer was a highly respected but controversial figure.

Acknowledgments

For many of the insights in this biography, I am indebted to a score of Bonhoeffer disciples. Towering above them all is Dr. Eberhard Bethge, a former fellow pastor in London and Bonhoeffer's definitive biographer and literary executor, as well as friend, confidant, and nephew-in-law. Bethge devoted three decades of love and labor to gathering materials about his former mentor. In turn, Theodore Gill's work provides unusually gifted color, imagination, enthusiasm, and synthesis. Sabine Leibholz, Dietrich's twin sister, offers rich detail about the family relationships. Mary Bosanquet gathered her lively account in part while living with various survivors. Martin Bailey's superb picture album of the Bonhoeffer era arouses one's nostalgia for the way things really were. I am also grateful to the firms of Harper and Row and the Christian Kaiser Verlag, which have kindly authorized the use of copyrighted material.

Page 75: Dietrich Bonhoeffer, *Gesammelte Schriften,* vol. 1 (Munich: Christian Kaiser, 1965–69), 23.

Page 82: Bonhoeffer, *Gesammelte Schriften,* 1:134.

Page 86: Eberhard Bethge, *Dietrich Bonhoeffer: Man of Vision, Man of Courage* (New York: Harper & Row, 1970), 177.

Page 139: Bonhoeffer, *Gesammelte Schriften,* 1:320.

Page 140: Dietrich Bonhoeffer, *Ethics* (New York: Macmillan, 1964), 3.

Page 142: Bethge, *Dietrich Bonhoeffer*, 585.

Page 168: Wolf-Dieter Zimmermann, *I Knew Dietrich Bonhoeffer* (New York: Harper & Row, 1966), 232.

Quotations of copyrighted materials and personal translations of German originals by permission of the various publishers.

1

"Naked Came I upon the Earth"

The weeks before the hanging had been filled with calm hope. Dietrich Bonhoeffer was only 39 years old and genuinely in love for the first time in his life. The awakening of spring always had brought him a kind of pagan delight, perhaps too primitive for a professor of theology. From the woods around the ruins of his castle prison at Flossenbürg, he could smell the nectar of blossoming linden and hawthorn. At dusk he could hear the nightingales, a pleasant change from the constant rumble of bombs that had been his melody in Berlin. At dawn came the lilting call of mating cuckoos.

For exactly two years, the Third Reich had been playing cat and mouse with Dietrich. Now the Gestapo had solid proof—proof that this professor of theology was involved with those who had plotted the death of Adolf Hitler. After 18 months in the rather lenient military prison at Tegel and four more under the stricter watch of the Gestapo on Prinz Albrecht Strasse, Dietrich now had arrived at the slave labor camp at Flossenbürg. This was usually the end of the line.

Realistically Dietrich's chances for avoiding the hangman's noose were slim, but there still was one thin strand of hope. Off to the west rumbled the thunder of American artillery, battering into the heartland of the Third Reich. From the east, hordes of *Volks*

Deutsch poured back into central Germany before the oncoming firepower of the Russians. Maybe, just maybe, the prison camp at Flossenbürg would be overrun by Americans or the line of communication from Berlin would be blasted to smithereens. If Dietrich could only survive through April, by May the Nazi empire might be sunk forever! Then he could once again roam his beloved forests, searching for mushrooms and strawberries.

The makeshift court martial, late at night on the Sunday after Easter, was a mere formality. Dietrich wasn't even present for the beginning of the trial. He had to be fetched from Schönberg, which was across the mountains from Flossenbürg. Among the accused were Admiral Canaris, General Oster, and Judge Advocate General Sack. The evidence against the plotters was conclusive. Every one of them had worked actively for the death of Hitler and the overthrow of the Third Reich. But the trial was only a formality; the verdict already was rendered. As a final act of revenge before he put a pistol to his own head, Hitler wanted all his opponents dead.

The extermination camp at Flossenbürg dominated the landscape. Built on the ruins of a medieval castle on the border between Germany and Czechoslovakia, it boasted a colorful history dating back to the Crusades. There, in the first gray light of dawn on Monday, April 9, 1945, the guards came to Dietrich's cell, rattled his door—just as they did the doors of the cells of Canaris, Oster, and Sack—and called, "Up! Off with the clothes!"

This was it. It was eight days after Easter, not a bad day to die—if one had to die. Naked as he awaited his death, Dietrich may have thought of a favorite hymn from the pen of Paul Gerhardt, which had been sung for generations by those facing death from plague, war, and famine. The hymn held special meaning for Dietrich because it had been the prayer his 6-year-old godson, Michael Dress, had sung when his Onkel Diet had been taken to prison. The second verse is most striking: "Naked came I upon the earth and naked shall I leave it."

In air perfumed with the blossoms of spring, Dietrich Bonhoeffer marched out under the lindens and firs with his guards. At the gallows, he knelt, prayed, slipped the noose over his neck, and awaited the springing of the trap. Within seconds of his fall, his body went limp, and only the joy of his spirit and the impact of his writings lives on.

At first the story of the Reverend Doctor Dietrich Bonhoeffer seems bizarre and improbable. He was singled out by his mother for her love and affection. He was indecisive. He had serious doubts about his faith. He lived through strange times—the days of Kaiser Wilhelm, the Weimar Republic, and the Third Reich. Yet Dietrich Bonhoeffer's life appears to be not only logical and orderly, but warm and idealistic and also remarkably fruitful and active.

To those who knew Dietrich as a child, it seemed unlikely that he would achieve great things. He had trouble coming to terms with himself and his world. Decisions came hard for him, and once he had considered every facet and worked things out, he was still not sure. His world always seemed too complex, too unreliable, too changeable—not at all like the warmth and understanding he knew from his mother. Perhaps he also was overshadowed by the outstanding achievements of his father and grandfathers and no less by those of his older brothers.

In his teens, Dietrich was considered a good pianist and composer and nearly devoted his life to music. But among the many amazing facts of Bonhoeffer's life was his choice to become a pastor and theologian. His family was not a church-going one. Although they said their prayers and listened to the Bible, largely at his mother's urging, Dietrich's psychiatrist father and his scientist brothers were disappointed to see him study theology. But in addition to goldsmithing, law, science, psychology, music, and painting, love of theology also ran in the Bonhoeffer line. In fact, one of Dietrich's grandfathers had served as Kaiser Wilhelm's chaplain. Once he chose his career, though, Dietrich met early success as a professor and theologian, with six books to his credit at the time of his death.

Dietrich Bonhoeffer did not look like a professor of theology. He was a big man, well over six feet tall, an athlete, round in the face, almost boyish. He had his mother's blue eyes and blond hair. He kept himself trim in a way that would have shocked the typically reserved professors in Germany—by swimming and playing tennis with his students. His physical conditioning eventually would help him to survive the rigors of prison life.

For a man who grew up before the age of the airplane, Dietrich did a remarkable amount of traveling. During his university days, he spent a term in Rome and North Africa. As an exchange student, he studied in New York. He preached in Cuba and lectured in Mexico City. He served a year's vicarage in Barcelona and, like Ernest Hemingway, became something of an aficionado of the bullring. For two years, Dietrich was a pastor in London. Three times he tried to join an ashram of Mahatma Gandhi in India. He traveled endlessly for the World Alliance of Churches—Denmark, Sweden, England, Germany, Switzerland, France, Scotland, Bulgaria.

How could a boy who had almost never warmed the seat of a pew grow up to preach in Berlin's most illustrious pulpits? How could a young theologian who hated war and fled to America rush home and apply for a chaplaincy just before the Nazi panzers trampled Poland? How could a preacher volunteer to work as a spy for the German *Wehrmacht?* How could a professor of theology plot to blow up Hitler? Despite his inability to arrive quickly at unassailable answers, of one thing Dietrich was quite certain. Not as a politician, not as a humanitarian, but strictly on moral grounds, he was willing to stake his life to fight Hitler.

So it was that in the first months of 1945, as World War II was rapidly drawing to a close and Germany was being pounded out of existence, Dietrich was shuttled under a rain of bombs from Berlin to Buchenwald to Schönberg to Flossenbürg. In the disruptions of wartime travel, he almost missed his own court martial. And even as he tried to cheer up other high-ranking prisoners by celebrating informal Easter services, his dark night on earth was coming to an end.

2

Marked for Greatness?

The Bonhoeffer clan had its roots in the Netherlands at Nymwegen. They always had been wealthy burghers, just below nobility. In 1513, Caspar von Bonhoeffer left Holland to escape the religious oppression that climaxed when Charles V was elected Holy Roman Emperor. Honest Dutchmen had never been fond of the Spanish throne nor its repressive brand of religion.

The traditional German home of the Bonhoeffers was the free city of Schwäbisch Hall in Württemberg. Originally goldsmiths, the family branched out to become doctors, lawyers, judges, professors, and preachers. Even in the rich city of Schwäbisch Hall, the Bonhoeffers were citizens of substance. To this day, despite the destruction of war after war, the Bonhoeffer burial sites in St. Michael's Church still mark the family as an important one: Life-size statues of saints and angels, oil portraits of half a dozen ancestors, marble columns and brass plaques, rich ornaments in gold and ivory—all in the best rococo style—grace the church and the crypts.

The Napoleanic invasion of 1806 broke up this idyll of rich medieval burghers and scattered the Bonhoeffer family. One hundred years later, however, Schwäbisch Hall remained something of a romantic shrine for Dietrich. He loved to visit the old patrician houses and climb their gabled stairways, finger the gold and pearl brooches that were family heirlooms, and eat the spiced cookies so characteristic of Swabia.

Dietrich's parents were of a generation that had seen Germany's birth as a nation. In the Franco-Prussian War of 1870, Otto von Bismarck, the Iron Chancellor, finally had brought together what had long been a strange jumble of independent duchies and kingdoms, making the new Germany equal with Great Britain and France.

Dietrich was born on February 4, 1906, the sixth of eight children. The eight children—Karl-Friedrich, Walter, Klaus, Ursula, Christine (also called Christel), twins Dietrich and Sabine, and Susanne were all born within a single decade, close enough in age to know one another well. Karl-Friedrich became a physicist of considerable reputation, Walter a naturalist, and Klaus a lawyer. Three of the four girls married lawyers, and Susanne wed a pastor.

The Bonhoeffer family had ancient and respected roots, and each child came to know and love the family's history. Dietrich's paternal grandfather, Friedrich Bonhoeffer, had long served as president of the Tübingen High Court and had a reputation as a strict law-and-order man. Dietrich's paternal grandmother, Julie, came from a more liberal family. Even as a grand old lady in her 90s, she thought nothing of walking through a cordon of storm troopers blocking off a Jewish store.

On Dietrich's mother's side, there also was ample reason to be proud of family heritage. His maternal grandfather, Karl von Hase, had been chaplain to Kaiser Wilhelm. In a sermon at the royal chapel at Potsdam, Pastor von Hase publicly objected to the emperor calling the French a "pack of dogs." This outspokenness cost him his appointment as chaplain, and he wound up professor of church history at the University of Breslau. Dietrich's maternal grandmother, Clara von Hase, born a von Kalckreuth and a countess, brought culture to the family. Her father and brother were two of Germany's best-known painters. She had studied piano with Klara Schumann and Franz Liszt.

Dietrich Bonhoeffer's father, Karl, was a professor of psychiatry in Breslau, on the Oder River, now a part of Poland. Dietrich spent the first six years of his life in a huge mansion in a forest of birch trees situated next door to the mental hospital in Scheitniger Park. The staff included a cook, a housemaid, a parlor maid, a governess, a French governess, a chauffeur, a receptionist, and a gardener. Dietrich's mother insisted on having a schoolroom, and his father set aside one room as a zoo where the children could keep lizards, snakes, rabbits, squirrels, guinea pigs, and pigeons. The garden was big enough for ice-skating, cave digging, and tent pitching, and it included an orchard and a tennis court.

Like most prosperous families, the Bonhoeffers owned a summer home. Theirs was at Wolfelsgrund. The woods there were as remote and as dense as those described in "Hansel and Gretel." Often with no supervision except that of the governesses, the Bonhoeffer youngsters clambered up the hunting towers, watched the deer come out to feed, gathered wild strawberries, and told each other haunted stories of the *Walpurgisnacht*, where the witches traditionally gathered on the night of April 30, on the highest mountain of the Hartz range, to build bonfires, dance, and offer sacrifices.

Yet life in the Bonhoeffer home was not without order and discipline. Although he was a busy man, Karl Bonhoeffer always reserved time for his children. He tried to spend some time with each child every day. He frequently skated, played tennis, and hiked with them. Most of all, he enjoyed talking with them. He wanted their thoughts and words to be well reasoned, not flighty or hasty. Although he was less cordial than his wife, Karl Bonhoeffer was such a rock of dependability that the children never hesitated to take a problem to him. To some degree, his training as a psychiatrist spilled over into his relationships with his children.

Dietrich's mother, Paula, was the more dominant of the two parents. It was she who insisted on having a classroom and teaching her children personally, though it meant she had to earn a proper license. It was she who invited other children to the classes. In most ways she was more strict than her husband. When one of the toddlers dropped a toy on a dirty floor, she had no compunctions about throwing it away. In fact, Paula Bonhoeffer was almost too fastidious about dirt. Her floors had to sparkle. The bedding had to be sunned and aired daily. She would not tolerate dust. In a hotel or on a train, she scrubbed the wash basin with antiseptic, which she carried in her bag.

Before Dietrich turned 6 years old, his parents moved to Berlin. There his father took an endowed chair as senior professor of neurology and psychiatry. For one who was not a disciple of Freud or Jung, this was a high honor. In the city, the brood of young Bonhoeffers, with their ancient roots in Swabia, Thuringia, and Pomerania, became Berliners through and through, taking advantage of the museums, galleries, theaters, and schools the capital city provided.

As at Breslau, the family did not at first buy a home, but lived in rented quarters. Karl Bonhoeffer found an old mansion near the zoo in Bellevue. With the narrowest of windows overshadowed by tall trees, the house was as gloomy as a prison. An open courtyard separated the reception rooms from the living quarters. Yet Bellevue was considered an address of considerable prestige—the address one would expect of a leading psychiatrist. In fact, the gardens overlooked those of the royal palace.

As he learned to know the city, Karl Bonhoeffer came to like the woods and lakes of the western suburbs best—areas of the city where many of the university professors lived. After three years, he bought a delightful town house in the suburb of Grunewald. The property was not much smaller than a country estate. The house stood on nearly an acre of land and boasted an orchard of apple, pear, and cherry trees. Three-and-a-half stories high, the house provided gracious shelter for Karl Bonhoeffer's study, his consulting rooms, his family, his staff of as many as seven servants, and during vacation time, as many as a dozen relatives and guests.

The choice rooms for family fun seem to have been the dining room and the living room. The surviving Bonhoeffers still have many photographs showing the glories of those two rooms. In the dining room, the parquet flooring was polished daily. The table could seat as many as 20. Paula Bonhoeffer's grandfather, Stanislas von Kalckreuth, who was a professional artist, designed the sideboard. Its serpentine pillars, inlays, and frieze made it look like a Greek temple. Dietrich's sisters recalled that the younger Bonhoeffers liked to climb to the top of this massive oak sideboard, lie eight feet in the air, and gaze out at the comings and goings of cooks and maids.

The reception room was no less grand. The largest grand piano made by Bechstein was not dwarfed by the equally massive furniture and oriental carpets that filled the room. The walls were as crowded with paintings as those of an art gallery. In addition to family portraits, there were huge landscapes of the Alps from the brushes of Dietrich's great-grandfather and great-great-grandfather, Stanislas and Leopold von Kalckreuth, both of whom had paintings in museums all across Europe.

All around him, the young Dietrich was surrounded by the impressive accomplishments of his ancestors—whether in art, medicine, science, or theology. In a sense, this was a challenge, but also something of a threat. When he grew up, would he be able to measure up? Was he also marked for greatness?

3

An Enchanted Childhood

Among the eight Bonhoeffer children, the three oldest were boys. Of the next five, however, Dietrich was the only boy sandwiched among four girls. Perhaps for this reason, he became his mother's favorite, was too much singled out, and was almost smothered by her love and discipline. Of the whole brood, Dietrich alone was blond, wavy-haired, and blue-eyed—Nordic like his mother.

Like that of most upper-class boys, Dietrich's schooling was strictly classical. In the fall of 1913, at the age of 7, Dietrich graduated from the home classroom, where he had been taught by his mother and two governesses, and enrolled at the Friedrich Werder Gymnasium. He was so shy, he could not bear to walk to school alone. Yet he rebelled at any thought of showing fear. His father worked out a compromise. On the opposite side of the street, a governess would walk a half-block behind him.

Two sisters who long served the family as governesses had a special influence on the young Dietrich. These were Maria and Katie Horn. Both had been trained in the religious teachings of the Moravian Brethren at Herrnhut, a school Frau Bonhoeffer also had attended briefly as a girl. The roots of this pietistic group went back to the teachings of John Hus in the 1400s, undergoing a renaissance under Count von Zinzendorf in the 1700s. These *Herrnhüter* were simple, hardworking, Bible-reading folk on the right wing of the Lutheran church. They thought Scripture-reading and home devotions as important as going to church.

The affable Horn sisters were a considerable influence on the Bonhoeffer children. Pictures show them smiling, dressed in the black-and-white dresses of their calling, joining in family parties, kicking a soccer ball, climbing into a deer blind, and scrambling over the dunes of the Baltic. Mother and governesses even dressed in the same black-and-white outfits, though Frau Bonhoeffer's fabrics were finer and her cuffs and collars were of the best lace. The Horn sisters were somewhat more pious in their beliefs than Frau Bonhoeffer, and the older boys pooh-poohed some of the Bible stories they told. Frau Bonhoeffer herself usually took over the teaching of religion, often using colored pictures of the life of Christ.

From their cradles onward, the Bonhoeffer children were instilled with a strong love for music. For them the German tradition of the *musikalischer Abend*, an evening a week when the family stayed home and made music together, was a living reality. For birthdays, christenings, or anniversaries, three or four of the children usually performed musically, either singing or playing. One favorite was Haydn's "Toy Symphony," lasting only a few minutes but with the four traditional movements of a full-blown symphony. This gave them the chance to tootle away as boisterously as they liked with toy trumpets, whistles, drums, and even the call of a cuckoo.

Although all the youngsters were reasonably good at music—singing, piano, violin, cello, flute—Dietrich was clearly in a class far above his brothers, who as young men no longer practiced seriously. Perhaps he had no more talent than they, but the special encouragement of his mother instilled in Dietrich a desire to achieve, to excel, and to some degree to be what his older brothers were not: a wise and sensitive humanitarian, like Frau Bonhoeffer's own brothers and father. By the age of 10, Dietrich could play a competent Mozart and Haydn, and by the age of 12, he could play Beethoven and Brahms. His mother and sisters demonstrated their affection for him by asking him to accompany them when they sang, though they were all reasonably good pianists themselves. At the keyboard Dietrich seemed to be less anxious and forgot his natural shyness. He memorized several psalms for his mother and later set them to music for her.

Dietrich enjoyed his greatest freedom at the summerhouse at Friedrichsbrunn. The lodge, once the home of a forester, came to mean as much to the younger Bonhoeffers as Wolfelsgrund had to the older ones. Friedrichsbrunn lay southwest of Berlin at the edge of a dense fir forest in the Harz Mountains. Dr. Bonhoeffer could seldom leave his practice for more than a week or two at a time, but mother and children, governesses and maids, cousins, uncles, and aunts all piled into the primitive country house.

The mystic lure of the forest lies deep in the heart of every child, but especially in the heart of a German child. The stories of Hansel and Gretel, the Brothers Grimm, and Ludwig Tieck all focus on the magic of larches and firs. In the forest near their summerhouse at Friedrichsbrunn, Dietrich and his twin, Sabine, discovered a clearing in the forest, which they named the witches' dance floor. Even in the woods. Dietrich remained continually the student, trying to learn everything there was to know. With the aid of Klaus, Dietrich learned the German and Latin names of almost everything that inhabited the forest, whether a thrush, a beetle, a lichen, a chipmunk, a hawk, a mushroom, or a roebuck.

From the peaks of the hills, young Bonhoeffer would lie in the grass and survey the world around him: the Thuringian Forest, the mountains of the Weser, the sudden outburst of a summer storm, the magic hues of sunrise, the mystic gray of the beeches, the swallows motionless on an updraft, or the pellets of fur an owl spits out when it has eaten a mole.

For the simple folk of Friedrichsbrunn, the Bonhoeffers made good summer guests. Often a maid arrived first, traveling from Berlin via train. She would help the caretaker's wife put the lodge in order. The caretaker mowed the meadow and raked the hay. Then the family arrived, sometimes together, sometimes in smaller groups, clip-clopping the four miles from the station in a horse cart.

It was during one of these glorious vacations in the Harzgebirge that the joys of family togetherness were shattered by World War I. Archduke Franz Ferdinand, heir to the Austro-Hungarian Empire, fell to an assassin's bullet in June 1914. The Triple Alliance of Germany, Austria, and Italy faced the Triple Entente of Britain, France, and Russia. In six weeks, all Europe was aflame.

Dietrich Bonhoeffer was 8 years old that summer. He listened eagerly to the bright-eyed talk of his brothers. He asked his grandparents to mail clippings; news was hard to come by in the forest. Dr. Bonhoeffer tried to dampen the children's enthusiasm, especially that of Christel, who chattered excitedly about the glories of battle.

For the Bonhoeffers, the war brought many changes. Refugees—Germans who for centuries had lived in Poland or the Ukraine—fled from the Russian front. One of these clans was quartered with the Bonhoeffers in that Grunewald mansion big enough to be a barracks. There the newcomers lived quietly in ground-floor rooms off the garden, a constant source of stories.

Almost from the start there was scarcity and rationing. The lawns at Wangenheimstrasse quickly became a vegetable garden. Dr. Bonhoeffer appointed Dietrich "messenger and food scout." It was he who visited the markets so the cook and the maid would know where to find potatoes and eggs and what the prices would be. The Bonhoeffers bought goats, more for the milk and cheese than for the meat. A flock of laying hens also settled in. Extra fruits and vegetables came from the huge rectory garden of Uncle Hans von Hase. Trips to Friedrichsbrunn became a chance to scrounge for food from the countryside. From the forest, Dietrich gathered a year's supply of mushrooms, strawberries, and lingenberries, drying them for the winter table.

Summer holidays were also the time when Hans von Hase, Dietrich's uncle, subtly encouraged his godson to consider becoming a pastor. No doubt Hans had been persuaded to undertake this task not a little by his sister, Dietrich's mother. Yet Dietrich was far from making up his mind about anything. His casual interest in the ministry was a cry for independence from the dominance of his father, mother, and brothers, but at the same time, it was an unacknowledged yielding to the dreams of his mother. Dietrich was not nearly so interested in science as a profession as the rest of his family. His father and brothers were all highly competent, all making a mark in the world, and the family circle of friends came from the highest levels of government and university. On every side, Dietrich felt pressured to compete. If only he could find one area where he could outstrip them all.

He had long discussed his religious feelings with Sabine. Perhaps because of his mother, perhaps because of Katie Horn, he liked best the spirited hymn tunes that came from the 18th century, pietist songs such as "Jesus, Lead Thou On" or "Jesus, Thy

Blood and Righteousness." These he called red hymns. He was less moved by black hymns, the classical and more stately chorales of traditional Lutheranism, such as "Now Thank We All Our God" or "Praise to the Lord, the Almighty."

In a sense, Dietrich also was becoming something of a mystic. He liked to lie awake at night, focusing on a phosphorescent cross. His continuing meditations on death were more like those of a medieval hermit than those of a preteen. Most of all, he focused on his need to be independent, his compulsion to achieve. He was almost desperate about finding new worlds to conquer.

Frau Bonhoeffer was mildly pietistic and her husband mildly agnostic. The family did not attend church regularly, even at the major festivals of Christmas and Easter. Yet the circle of Dr. Bonhoeffer's friends included not only scientists and physicians, but also theologians. For christenings and weddings, the family turned not to the parish pastor, but to Frau Bonhoeffer's brother Hans. What religious ceremonies there were took place at home, not in church. Even festivals such as Christmas and Easter were celebrated in the home, not in church. On Good Friday, however, in the popular German pattern, the family often sat in church for a musical presentation of the passion in the versions of Johann Sebastian Bach or Heinrich Schuetz.

The Evangelical Church of Germany was a peculiar blend of Protestantism. Growing largely from the teachings of Martin Luther but avoiding the Lutheran name, it also incorporated some of the doctrines of John Calvin. Some congregations and some districts were strongly Lutheran; others were strongly Reformed. The regional churches of some 28 states were all independent, each going its own way. In 1817, Kaiser Wilhelm had tried to solve the problem by ordering a single Prussian Union, a forced attempt at conformity, but that only made matters worse.

In any case, Frau Bonhoeffer developed her own church under her own roof. As helpers, she recruited the Horn sisters, Maria and Katie. Both assisted her with hymns, psalms, Bible stories, and commandments. Her church really came alive at Advent and Christmas. It was then that she instilled in her brood a kind of family religion they never forgot. Years later, from the prison cell at Tegel, Dietrich brought tears to his mother's eyes by reminding her how joyful she had made all their Christmases.

Although Saturday was the usual night for "musical evenings," in Advent the family often sat at the table singing carols and hymns. Especially popular were "O Come, O Come, Emmanuel" and "Lift Up Your Heads, Ye Mighty Gates." This was also the time when the children made one another's Christmas presents. While the youngsters worked with their hands, their father usually read aloud from the tales of Hans Christian Andersen. There was also a reading from Scripture, usually by Frau Bonhoeffer, candles to light, and Advent calendars to open. Throughout the evening, the family munched on cookies, candy, and stollen—all homemade—and gulped down pots of chocolate.

On Christmas Eve, the family, including the maids and governesses in their black-and-white uniforms, gathered in a huge circle in the parlor. Then Frau Bonhoeffer, in a black velvet gown with white lace, took over. Her musical voice was gifted equally for singing or for reading. Sometimes the lessons were of her own composition, but they always included the story of Christ's annunciation and birth from Matthew and Luke. Hymns and carols were interspersed with Christmas prayers. Usually her eyes filled with tears, as did those of her children, more to see their mother moved than by their own feelings.

All this took place by candlelight. Dr. Bonhoeffer also took part, reading and singing with the rest, out of admiration for a wife who could do so much for his children. It was usually he who lit the candles on the Christmas tree, just before the gift-giving, while the younger children danced around singing "O Tannenbaum."

Similar festivities marked the New Year and Easter. The family traditions for New Year's Eve—St. Sylvester's Day—always included a festive meal, usually of goose, and the telling of fortunes. On this night, Frau Bonhoeffer read Psalm 90: "LORD, thou hast been our dwelling place in all generations." Just before the church bells rang at midnight, the family sang one of those Paul Gerhardt hymns most Germans thought more inspired than even the Bible, "Come Now with Praise and Singing."

Daily the younger children said the table prayers. Those at bedtime, supervised either by Frau Bonhoeffer or one of the governesses, were always said in the dark to prevent the youngsters from grandstanding. For the little ones the routine was usually "Müde bin ich," the German counterpart of "Now I Lay Me Down to Sleep." Next came the Lord's Prayer and one verse of a hymn of the child's choosing, which was sung from memory. All the children memorized hymns by the score.

Each child was discouraged from taking himself or herself too seriously, even in religion. The Bonhoeffer ethos was that one should show pride in appearance, manners, and courtesy but even more in character, truthfulness, and honesty. Sometimes Dietrich's mother worried that she and the governesses had made her youngest son fear religion. He was forever fascinated by the subject of death, talking about it, writing about it, asking his father to predict when a particular patient would die. Every night he checked to make sure his twin had said her prayers for fear one of them might die during the hours of darkness.

At age 12, Dietrich left Sabine and graduated to his own bedroom. This was a symbol of growing up, a loss of childhood. Just the year before, he had lost the wavy, shoulder-length hair of his boyhood, keeping it much later than the other boys. Except in the summer, he gave up his *lederhosen*. He was now nearly ready for confirmation. Dietrich had finally left the magic kingdom of an enchanted childhood and come of age.

4

Crossing the Rubicon

At the start of World War I, Dietrich Bonhoeffer was 8-1/2 years old; at its close, he was nearly 13. As a boy, he had played with the royal princes and loved the burnished brass and polished boots of the Grenadier Guards. Yet as the war drew to a climax, he no longer thought the military so glamorous. In 1917, Karl-Friedrich and Walter reached draft age and in 1918, Klaus. The family celebrated the departure of the two older sons with festivities: a friendly meal; a time of singing, toasting, and speech-making; then a party to see them off at the station. As they left, Frau Bonhoeffer ran the length of the platform, waving her good-byes and blessings.

In Belgium in the spring of 1918, Walter suffered a shrapnel wound. He wrote cheerfully that the surgeons were probing for shell fragments. Five days later, he died. That autumn, Karl-Friedrich also was wounded but less seriously. For Frau Bonhoeffer, the death of Walter brought on a nervous breakdown. She lived next door under the roof of kindly neighbors for nearly a year, much of the time in bed. Especially for the three youngest children, those were difficult days. Dietrich later wrote of them as the saddest of his life.

The last years of World War I brought drastic changes throughout Germany. The country no longer basked in the conquests of von Clausewitz and Bismarck but was on the verge of anarchy. Food, morale, and public health all disappeared. Feelings against the emperor ran high. The political troubles first sprouted on the eastern front, borrowed from the populist variety of communism based on the writings of Karl Marx that was breaking out in the Russian armies.

In German intellectual circles, too, communism held considerable appeal. Like most of their contemporaries, the older Bonhoeffers had read Karl Marx. Although not supportive of communism, they were also lukewarm toward the monarchy. Like many Germans, the Bonhoeffers were actively looking for a change in government. Late in October 1918, just before the armistice on November 11, President Woodrow Wilson of the United States announced that the overthrow of Kaiser Wilhelm would not be enough. The Allies demanded unconditional surrender, along with huge reparations in money and territory. When the Armistice was declared and the Kaiser abdicated, Klaus served him as an orderly and witnessed the event.

The political troubles of 1918 made an impression on 12-year-old Dietrich, who often heared gunshots on the way to school and read of suicides and assassinations in the newspapers. These times stirred in him a lasting interest in practical politics. Twice the communists tried to take over the Grunewald subway station, but they were beaten back. Even in defeat, however, Berlin was proving to be what Klaus always claimed: the *liveliest* city in the world.

All these troubles—the death of a son, the breakdown of a mother, the resignation of an emperor, the uprising of the communists—would have brought even more disruption to the household on Wangenheimstrasse had it not been for the steady hand of Dr. Karl Bonhoeffer. During his wife's illness, he found even more time to be a generous and understanding father. Not an emotional man, he taught more by quiet example than by sermonizing. With the help of the governesses, he tried to prepare each child for the life that lay ahead.

Every New Year, Dr. Bonhoeffer recorded a kind of running history of the family. He noted just enough about the outside world to provide a good overview of what the Bonhoeffers were thinking, first with images of an imperial Berlin, then a republican one, and finally a socialist one. This was a Berlin of street politics, of cabaret brawls, of Bolshevik assassins, of clashes in the government, but it was also a Berlin that doted on music and painting and ballet and poetry.

Already as a young boy, Dietrich showed an interest in becoming a clergyman, encouraged along the way by his mother especially. His brothers tended to laugh at his dream, saying the church was old and decaying. This only annoyed him. If what they said was really true—and Dietrich thought it might be—the church needed good men to give it energy and direction. His special feelings for his mother always kept Dietrich close to the clerical side of the family. Her brother Hans, father, and grandfather had made distinguished careers for themselves in the church. Moreover, the three-year gap in age between Dietrich and the next oldest child was now becoming significant. The four older children were off at the university or actively considering careers and marriage, almost a separate generation. Dietrich was carefully considering his future.

Dietrich's dream to be a pastor was unusual for someone with so few practical ties to the church. Yet the Bonhoeffers had not completely flouted convention. They did christen their children, if only at home, and they did send them to church for religious instruction. So when their turn came, Dietrich and his sister Sabine also traipsed off for confirmation classes.

Because of his mother's tutoring, Dietrich was a year younger than most of his classmates. He had, of course, plenty of time to choose his life's direction. At 13, the year after the war, he showed a fleeting interest in boy scouting. He liked the hiking and the nature study, but he soon tired of the marching and drilling, all of which was conducted on Sunday mornings. His older brothers teased him that he was trying to become a war hero the easy way, insisting that their generation had done the real fighting.

Dietrich was more moody and introspective than his brothers. Sometimes, in the middle of a lively conversation, he withdrew into a trance and became lost in his own thoughts. Once when he and Klaus were invited to a party, he declined on the grounds that it was Lent, a response that shocked both his hosts and his brother because he had never before taken note of Lent.

In school, Dietrich read the usual German, Latin, and Greek of the classical *gymnasium*: Goethe, Schiller, Hesse, and Hofmansthal; Virgil, Horace, Julian, and Plotinus; Plato, Homer, Euripides, and Aristophanes. He wrote playlets for the family and the class. He did not read theology, though he was on good terms with neighboring theologians. He seemed almost to dread finally making up his mind about a career, especially one in theology. On occasion, he wondered if religion ever *did* anything. It seemed too philosophical, too impractical. Like his brothers, he toyed with the notion that the church really had died in the Middle Ages and been given an honorable burial.

His mother and father suggested that Dietrich consider a career in music. As a pianist, composer, and arranger, he showed more talent than any of their other children. They consulted a professional from Vienna, Leonid Kreuzer. The artiste was eminently practical. Dietrich obviously had talent, but did he also have the will? At 14, talent alone would not make a career.

When he was 15 and in his final year at the gymnasium, Dietrich chose Hebrew as an elective. This tipped off his masters that he wanted to study theology. All students learned Greek, but only future pastors bothered with Hebrew. Dietrich must have been unusually sensitive about his choice, both with his family and with his classmates. Thirteen years later, in a letter to a friend, he revealed how dramatically he had experienced the situation. His conversion experience was as deep as St. Augustine's or Charles Wesley's.

Apparently the "crisis" came during a Greek class on the very first day of the term. The master was inquiring what the students wanted to be. He called on Dietrich, and the young man answered shyly, with a distinct blush, "A theologian." Dietrich recalled that he was too embarrassed either to stand or to say the usual "sir," an indication that he was emotionally tense. The instructor excused him from translating for the day and commented amiably that with such a career ahead of him, he would face many surprises and challenges.

That little incident burned its way into Dietrich's mind. That night he recalled a quotation from Friedrich von Schiller. The German dramatist and poet had written that when a man overcomes his weaknesses, he becomes godlike. Somehow Dietrich felt godlike that day. He no longer felt like the family weakling. He had publicly announced his intention to become a pastor. "I shall study theology. ... I have said so, and they all heard it. There is no more retreat." It was as if he had crossed his Rubicon. He felt as if he had just taken his ordination vows.

36

5

1923

At 17 years of age, Dietrich graduated from the gymnasium and was ready for the university. On the one hand, he was a scholar and a recluse, as the thesis for his *abitur*, or graduation dissertation, on Catullus and Horace as lyric poets demonstrated. On the other hand, the side of his personality he often preferred to show was that of a man of action, a swimmer, a tennis player, and a runner. He acted more like a scholar, but he looked more like an athlete. His eagerness to be a part of the real world was distorted by the very confusion he experienced within that world: political upheaval, economic disturbances, and family adversity.

By the year 1923, Frau Bonhoeffer had recovered much of her former vitality. Again the huge mansion on Wangenheimstrasse sparkled with the lights and candles of fancy dress balls, musical evenings, and amateur theatricals. More than once, Dr. Bonhoeffer and his wife costumed themselves as Wotan and Freya, figures in German mythology. Dietrich sometimes dressed as Cupid and shot paper arrows of love at unsuspecting guests. Dr. Bonhoeffer was not too reserved to don the livery of a butler and serve his unsuspecting guests champagne.

The four older children grew up quickly and flew from the family nest. They had been an unusually happy brood, roughhousing, sparring, goading one another. Karl-Friedrich, the eldest, was 24 years old the year Dietrich graduated from the gymnasium. Already a brilliant scientist, Karl-Friedrich had split the hydrogen atom and was soon to be invited to lecture in Russia and America, 20 years before there was an atom bomb. The youngest of the older girls, Christel, was already 20. Dietrich, Sabine, and Susanne, the younger three, sometimes felt left out. Sabine and Susanne thought of Dietrich as a kind of "knight on white horse," guarding and protecting them against the slings and arrows of an outrageous fortune, the mature world of the grown-ups. Perhaps they equated Dietrich with the famous statue in the cathedral at Bamberg. To this day, no one knows who the statue really represents, whether St. George, King Conrad, or Clement II, the only German ever to become pope.

Each of the children had grown independent over the years, even Dietrich who at 7 years of age had been reluctant to walk to school alone. At heart they were all explorers. On the way to Friedrichsbrunn, Dietrich often jumped off the train at Halberstadt or Quedlinburg to wander for hours through the cathedral and the half-timbered alleyways. He would then catch a later train to rejoin the family.

The strand of the Baltic was also a natural magnet. With their university friends, the four older Bonhoeffers often caught the train to one of the northern resorts for a day of sand and water. With Karl-Friedrich usually came his fiancée, Greta von Dohnanyi, the daughter of the famous composer. Often Dietrich would tag along and shepherd the two younger girls.

Often as not, Klaus played a game of beach ball with two budding young lawyers, Rüdiger Schleicher and Hans von Dohnanyi, Greta's brother. Ursula Bonhoeffer, brilliant and beautiful, singled out Rüdiger as a future husband, and Christel chose Hans. Tragically, of those three lawyers, only Klaus was to escape death at the hands of the Nazis, but his place would be taken by Dietrich. A fourth law student also began to come along. That was Gerhard Leibholz, a member of a Jewish family, who had taken a liking to 17-year-old Sabine. That he was able to flee Germany before the outbreak of the war spared him the fate of the others.

On their own or in the company of friends, the Bonhoeffer children constantly traveled. In medieval Germany, a young teenager first learned a trade as an apprentice, then traveled as a journeyman before becoming a master craftsman. Thus, travel was considered an important part of learning and maturing. For the Bonhoeffers, one favorite destination was always the family birthplace at Schwäbisch Hall. There the gurgling fountains and the geranium-filled window boxes always brought a sense of continuity and belonging, as if one's life were something more than that of a mere wanderer on earth.

Other favorite haunts also had family ties. One was the Alte Pinakothek at Munich. There, in wall-size splendor, hung the canvases of great-grandfather Count Stanislas von Kalckreuth, paintings of a glorious Alpenglow settling down over the mountains or a thunderhead pouring out buckets of rain on a mountain village. Only a shade less exciting were the paintings of his son, Count Leopold von Kalckreuth, in the museum at Hamburg. When young Bonhoeffers wanted a bit of travel, the paintings of their grandfather and great-grandfather always provided a good excuse for a trip.

For those who enjoyed a more rural setting, there was the country home of another grandparent: the Thuringian Forest and the town of Eisenach, where Johann Sebastian Bach had once been organist. Guarding nearby Wittenberg rose the Wartburg, the mighty fortress that had hosted a variety of guests such as St. Elizabeth, Martin Luther, and the Meistersinger of Wagner's opera. At Weimar there was a double tie. Always hospitable to things cultural, Weimar had once been the home of Franz Liszt, piano teacher of Grandma Klara von Hase. Weimar also was the town where great-grandfather Stanislas von Kalckreuth had founded a school for painters.

Fortunately, the house on Wangenheimstrasse was the family's natural gathering place, though the four older children were now off on their own. At a time when Germany was undergoing drastic change, the Bonhoeffer family at least was stable. Government in Germany was in turmoil, with democrats, communists, socialists, and monarchists struggling for power. Almost every week, the nation witnessed demonstrations and political murders. The French and British demands for war reparations from a country where people were still starving only increased the feeling of unrest. Germany could no longer meet its assessments. Its people had nothing left in the cash box for food.

Hoping to squeeze money out of the mines and smelters, France invaded the Ruhr. The people responded with passive resistance as the whole community laid down its tools. All this happened during 1923, the year Dietrich finished his schooling at the gymnasium. Life in Germany came almost to a standstill. Politicians of every stripe denounced France, condemned the Treaty of Versailles, and repudiated the burden of war reparations.

Germany seemed caught in a bottomless pit. The disturbances included an uprising in Munich by a house painter no one had previously heard of: Adolf Hitler. Eventually, under the leadership of President Gustav Stresemann, a new Germany slowly began to rise from the ashes of war, helped by the Dawes Plan, the Young Plan, and the Locarno Treaty. This finally set the pattern for the happy Germany Bonhoeffer was to know best, a quiet and peaceful time that was to prove such a contrast to the later violence of the Nazis.

What happened during that significant year of 1923 strongly affected Bonhoeffer as he settled in on his own at the university in Tübingen. The worst effect of the various disturbances was inflation. Money lost all value. To buy a loaf of bread, one needed a whole suitcase of marks. Bonhoeffer wrote home to report that his meals cost a billion marks each. Wiser students than he had contracted earlier to buy a book of meal tickets for the whole term for two and a half billion marks.

A more poignant story comes out of Dr. Bonhoeffer's diaries. For decades he had been saving money in annuities, and two of them matured in 1923. The sum was considerable—a hundred thousand marks, with a buying power of perhaps $25,000 in contemporary America. He had hoped to use the money to put the younger children through school. Instead, with inflation so wild, he thought he would at least enjoy a bitter joke. He would use the cash to buy ingredients for a punch of white wine and crushed strawberries called a Berliner Bowle. Unfortunately, inflation galloped on at such a speed that by the time he cashed the checks, he could buy only the strawberries. He had to use other money for the wine.

Even inflation was not without its silver lining. Those were the days when Sigmund Freud and the new psychiatry had caught the imagination of half the world. Dr. Bonhoeffer, convinced that the "gospel" coming out of Vienna was exaggerated beyond the limits of scientific evidence, was no Freudian. Nonetheless, he was Germany's leading psychiatrist and the natural magnet of many rich patients flocking to Berlin, especially from abroad. In exchange for a consultation, Dr. Bonhoeffer could collect priceless dollars and pounds. Only one patient, if a foreigner, sometimes meant several suitcases of devalued marks. At the peak of the inflation, he took a four-day holiday to Jena with his wife and another couple, paying fares, food, and hotel with the $4 fee from one consultation.

Even if they were unpleasant, the troubles Dietrich experienced in the early 1920s—inflation, political turmoil, lawlessness, assassinations, strikes—prepared him for the even greater upheavals a decade later when Hitler came to power.

6

University Days

For a typical German, leaving home and going off to the university is as mystical as listening for the siren song of the Lorelei maidens or remembering St. Boniface chopping down the sacred oak. The University of Tübingen was the alma mater of Dietrich's father and brothers. His sister Christel was a term or two ahead of him there, and together the two Bonhoeffers would bring a bit of youth and brightness to the life of their ever-spirited grandmother, Klara von Hase, whose deceased husband had once been the senior judge of the district.

Tübingen had long been one of Germany's five or six most famous universities. It is a pleasant old town in the rolling countryside north of the Swiss border. On the heights sits an old castle, the Twingia, and down in the valley flows the Neckar. As at Cambridge, the river provides students a chance to work off their high spirits by punting. The shallow-bottomed boats are pushed along with poles, which sometimes stick in the mud and dump the punter into the water.

At Tübingen, Dietrich thoroughly immersed himself in the study of theology. The Latin, Greek, and Hebrew he had learned at the gymnasium got him off to a good start. The Tübingen theological faculty was an able one, with scholars such as Schlatter, Heim, Rudolph, and Groos. His sister Christine suggested he also take a course or two in the natural sciences he had always loved, but Dietrich was too single-minded to waste time with anything but theology.

Perhaps because he thought it would please his father, Dietrich joined his father's fraternity, which was called the *Igel*, the Hedgehog. None of his older brothers had been members, arguing that the fraternity was taking part in too many political demonstrations. New pledges were called *Füchse*, or foxes. The senior classmen were *Burschen*, or fellows, and the alumni were *alte Herren*, or ancient gentlemen. The Igel's three-story fraternity house was built of stone and timber and looked almost like a cathedral. In student slang, it was called "the beer church." Like other young Germans, the members of the Igel talked politics, usually in the beer-drinking room that really was a "beer church."

The Igel was a "black" fraternity, not one of the ancient and honorable dueling societies that delighted in sword fighting and whose members proudly wore lifelong scars to mark their university days. A sword scar was thought to be public proof of one's courage, membership in an exclusive fraternity, and a university degree. Igel members made fun of the older traditions, reasoning that scars were not all that pretty, even if they were signs of manhood. Instead of the brightly colored caps and uniforms most fraternity men wore, the members of the Igel sported three shades of gray. Their cap was fashioned to look like a hedgehog and included a few quills. Dietrich, though a year or two younger than most of the other pledges, made many friends. Only a decade later did he understand why his two older brothers had refused to join. The Igel would be one of the first groups to support Hitler.

After World War I, Germany was allowed only a tiny standing army: a hundred thousand men, scarcely a good-size police force. After France had taken advantage of the situation by overrunning the Saar and the Ruhr in 1923, student organizations patriotically began secret military training. The whole membership of the Igel trooped off for such training.

In contrast to the regular army, called the Reichswehr, these irregular bands of students were called the Black Reichswehr. Usually they drilled on campus under veteran instructors, calling themselves the Ulm Rifles. When the Allied Control Commission sent observers, however, the students moved off-campus. Dietrich talked the situation over with his grandmother, who thought the Ulm Rifles innocent enough, especially in light of uprisings such as the Beer Putsch at Munich. Along with his companions, Bonhoeffer caught an early morning train for Ulm for four days of maneuvers. It was an unusual choice for a young man who already was thinking of himself as a pacifist, but Dietrich did not want to alienate his friends or be thought unconventional.

Apparently Dietrich showed little talent with a carbine and jackboots. The barracks were primitive and splintery, dirtier and more uncomfortable than even the summer home at Friedrichsbrunn. According to a family legend, Dietrich was ordered to scrub the floor with a toothbrush, lost his sense of humor, and angrily flung a pail out a window. He lasted only two days. The whole episode left him with a bitter dislike for the military. The army sergeants he met worried him. They were insensitive, ill-educated, and domineering—all the things an aristocrat disliked. He wrote his parents how happy he was to be back where the floors were clean, the beds sheeted, the tableware spotless, the baths hot, and the company civilized.

On the other hand, Dietrich does not seem to have been merely a bookworm. When the Neckar froze that winter, he demonstrated his skill as a figure skater. In Berlin, he had been overshadowed by the talents of Klaus and Karl-Friedrich, more finely boned and agile than he. But Dietrich was highly competent, far more skilled than most young athletes. One severe tumble, however, knocked him unconscious, and what was more ominous, he remained unconscious for days. To a psychiatrist such as Dr. Bonhoeffer, such a symptom indicated possible brain damage, and the two parents quickly caught a train to Tübingen. During a considerable period of convalescence, Dietrich enjoyed seeing his father relive old school days and his mother spend long afternoon teas with her mother.

The skating accident had a happy aftermath: a term in Rome. At first his parents were reluctant to let him go because he was only 17. In Berlin, his brother Klaus had just finished his law exams, however, and was also free to accompany his younger brother. Dietrich pleaded. Dr. Bonhoeffer made inquiries. In short order the plans were finalized. Dietrich would do a term in classical history and theology in Rome. There would be more sightseeing than anything else, but enough study to make the effort appear educational.

Klaus and Dietrich rode the train over the Brenner Pass early in April 1924, just in time to celebrate Holy Week and Easter in Rome. Aboard the coach, the two Bonhoeffer's met a fascinating young priest from Bologna, an Austrian. He offered to serve as a guide for all the events of *la santa semana*. Klaus and Dietrich naturally had different interests. Five years apart in age, one had just passed his bar exams and the other was a budding theologian. Klaus was more interested in classical and historical Rome and not at all averse to sitting and sipping cappuccino on the Via Veneto, trying to pick out the shapeliest girls. Dietrich also appreciated the classical world, but for the moment, he was more intrigued by the colorful rites of the Roman church, a subject new, strange, and fascinating.

Together the two brothers made the rounds of St. Peter's, the Colosseum, the Spanish Steps, the Trevi Fountain, the Vatican, the Villa Borghese. Dietrich was so moved that he recorded every detail in letters and his diary. He knew the Baedeker guidebook by heart. He stared at the tense splendor of the Laocoon statue and the massive durability of the Colosseum, which at that time was sprouting occasional cypresses and palm trees between the stones.

What moved Dietrich most was the sturdy faith he saw in those good Romans who were celebrating Holy Week. He wished his own faith could have been as strong. The Palm Sunday Mass at St. Peter's started the week's round. He had never seen so many monks and seminarians, all chanting the ancient plainsongs of Palestrina. In multicolored garb, and from every corner of the world, they reminded him of medieval pilgrims come to pay their respects to the graves of Peter and Paul. That evening, walking past the house of Keats and Shelley at the foot of the Spanish Steps, Dietrich succumbed to the beauty of Vespers at Trinita del Monte, a church whose majesty he later dreamed of in prison.

With his friendly priest to steer him and explain, Dietrich spent hours at the basilica of Santa Maria Maggiore. What caught his attention was the rite of confession. Despite his catechism training, he scarcely remembered what confession was about, the practice had fallen into such disuse among Lutherans. Now he watched old and young take their turns at the confessionals. It seemed so natural, so unforced, so much a way of life. Long lines of penitents quietly waited their turn, meditating and praying. In the past, Dietrich wrote in his diary, he had thought of confession as a teaching device. Now he saw it as a genuine form of worship. For these Romans, the priest seemed to have a direct channel to heaven, and the people acted not as if they were talking to a man, but to God. The color of the robes, the mystical darkness of the churches, the incense, the flickering of hundreds of candles, all this gave Dietrich a religious experience that was new and compelling. His feelings, though not his mind, struggled to be Catholic instead of a coldhearted Lutheran from the northlands.

On Good Friday, the one day when there is no Mass, Dietrich spent five hours at St. Peter's observing the dark-draped altar and the throngs paying reverence to the empty cross. On Easter Eve, he watched the ceremony of the new fire, the ancient ritual symbolizing Christ's escape from the tomb. From the joyful rites of Easter, he received a sprouting grain of wheat, a symbol of Christ who, like a kernel of wheat, spent three days in the earth before bursting forth, alive.

Holy Week in Rome had a dramatic effect on the young theologue. Perhaps his parents had been wise in sending Klaus, otherwise Dietrich might have joined a monastery. Klaus helped keep Dietrich's feet on the ground, visiting not only churches, but nightclubs, restaurants, and museums. Both young men knew enough Roman history to ferret out the Appian Way and the Forum and to check out the sites of the stories they had long studied. Dietrich was especially intrigued by the frescoes and mosaics of the early Christians, and he spent days crawling through the catacombs, lantern in hand, searching out ancient chapels and cemeteries. Klaus wearied of Rome more quickly and arranged an excursion to Sicily and—what was considerably more daring—a trip across the Mediterranean to Libya and into the Atlas mountains.

The two young men were not altogether sure this detour would meet with the approval of their parents in Berlin. They did have enough filial piety, however, to write home about the escapade once they were in North Africa but enough practicality not to ask permission to go. For 10 days, they lived in the desert, guests of a Bedouin sheik. Exactly what happened there, Klaus and Dietrich must have agreed never to tell, and neither ever talked or wrote about it. In any case, there was some kind of falling out between the sons of Germany and the sons of Islam, and Klaus and Dietrich left Tripoli as unwelcome guests.

At this point, Klaus headed to Berlin to start his law career. Dietrich stayed behind to catch up on the bookwork of his semester in Rome. In what library he worked, where he studied, or how the credits were arranged is somewhat vague. He fell so much in love with Italy that his mother wondered whether he might follow the footsteps of his grandfather, who had lived long in Rome, collected Italian paintings, and carved out a name as a famous scholar of early church history. Although Dietrich stretched out the Roman holiday to the last possible hour, he returned home to Wangenheimstrasse in mid-June, barely in time to enroll for the summer term. He had resolved to study theology at the nation's cultural center: the University of Berlin.

7

Berlin

The three-and-a-half years Dietrich lived at home and studied at the University of Berlin were perhaps the happiest and most stable of his life. He had seen enough of the world to know what he wanted. He was industrious enough and intelligent enough that studying was never a burden. He was under no great pressure. He enrolled at Berlin in June 1924 at the age of 18. In short sequence, he earned his bachelor's and doctoral degrees and his licentiate as a pastor. Shortly before Christmas 1927, 21-year-old Dietrich defended his doctoral thesis.

During Dietrich's year at Tübingen and Rome, things had changed drastically at the house on Wangenheimstrasse. Sabine had become engaged and gone off to the university at Breslau. His ties with his twin came to a natural end. Susanne, three years younger than Dietrich and the baby of the family, now took Sabine's place.

Since childhood, Dietrich had been something of a loner. He was too self-sufficient. Although he delighted in good conversation, he did not go out of his way to make friends. There were too many other interesting things to do. Unlike his brothers and sisters, he showed little interest in the opposite sex or in marrying. Perhaps he was too much dominated by his mother or too much involved in the intellectual world. He did spend many weeks at the country house with his cousin Hans. Frying bacon and eggs over the old wood stove, staying up nights with the novels of

Franz Werfel, talking politics, roaming the woods for mushrooms and nuts, all these Dietrich preferred to Berlin partying.

Yet Berlin was never bored or boring. Even if Dietrich had not yet developed real friendships, he was forever taking home some student or other. He singled out those with difficulties, those who, like himself, were lonely. This was probably a kind of therapy. He, too, felt alone and unloved, in need of psychological support, and his attempts to help others were quiet indicators of his own need.

Earlier in the century, Berlin might well have been the most exciting city in Europe, but after World War I, that honor passed to Paris or London. Nonetheless, there was seldom a week when Dietrich did not attend a symphony or an opera, a play or an exhibition. Intellectually and politically, Berlin had programs that matched those anywhere. In poetry, drama, and publishing, it demonstrated genuine flair, and after the quieter stay in Tübingen, Dietrich again found the city exciting.

Dietrich had come to be interested in theology in an odd way. Despite the scientific bent of his family, he threw himself into the study of religion more on the basis of personal need than of intellect. There was a certain emptiness in his life, a note of rebelliousness. He would prove to his brothers and father that he, too, could excel.

Like most Germans, Dietrich was awed by the tradition of Martin Luther. He even tried to work out the similarities between his own path to faith and that of Luther, as he later explained at considerable length in *Cost of Discipleship*. Luther, he wrote, had rediscovered grace. God saves human beings because He wants to, because of His grace in Christ, not because humans deserve it. As a young man not much older than Bonhoeffer, Luther also had made a pilgrimage to Rome. Unlike Bonhoeffer, Luther had hated the religious practices he found there, where people were trying to save themselves by their own good works, walking up the Sacred Stairs on their knees, saying daily rosaries, buying indulgences.

Despite Bonhoeffer's almost mystical words about Luther, whom he treated as reverently as if he were a saint, he also realized what had happened to the church since Luther. When faith alone counted, people grew lazy. They never became real disciples. Eventually faith vanished. To keep faith alive meant being a continuing disciple, like Peter or James or John, not a sit-at-home whose religion was an intellectual exercise.

With these convictions, Dietrich tackled the theological courses of the University of Berlin. The theology department was only about a century old, with less prestige than Marburg, Heidelberg, or Erlangen. The star of the faculty was an old and distinguished neighbor of the Bonhoeffers, Adolf von Harnack, who still held a few seminars. It was Harnack who persuaded Bonhoeffer to be not only a pastor, but a professor.

For course work, Dietrich chose classes taught by other members of the faculty. As Eberhard Bethge suggests, he may have been somewhat hesitant to submit himself to so overpowering and dominating a personality as von Harnack. Dietrich was probably most influenced by Reinhold Seeberg, for whom he wrote his thesis. From Seeberg, Dietrich also learned that the church should be socially and politically oriented, a point of view he would push during the Nazi takeover.

Two other teachers had a profound effect on the 18-year-old student. One was Karl Holl, who was perhaps the greatest Luther scholar of his generation. Although he died midway through Dietrich's stay at Berlin, he still had time to convey something deep and lasting about the great reformer, a sympathy and understanding Dietrich would never forget. The last of those who strongly influenced Dietrich was Adolf Deissmann. Still young, Deissmann was one of the most active ecumenicists in Germany. From him, Dietrich absorbed an enthusiasm for the work of Christian churches all over the world. Eventually the student would be even more active in the ecumenical movement than his master.

What Bonhoeffer learned at Berlin came not only from its own faculty, but from a young Swiss professor who had begun teaching at Göttingen—Karl Barth. The whole campus at Göttingen buzzed with talk about its new theological star. Barth could even excite Dietrich's cousin, Hans Christoph von Hase, who was not a theologian, but a physicist. Summarizing the role of Karl Barth as the major theological figure of the century might take as many thousands of pages as he himself used in his seemingly endless *Christian Dogmatics*. Barth flashed on the scene like a meteor, studied and taught throughout Germany, helped write the Barmen Confession that clearly condemned the anti-Christian character of the Third Reich, then returned to teach at his native Basel.

The theological movement Barth started has been labeled *Neo-Orthodoxy*, and his famous students, including Bultmann, Gogarten, Tillich, and Niebuhr, were tagged Barthians. Very simply, Barth tried to sweep away the theological debris that had accumulated for decades and to turn the church back to a pristine vision of an all-knowing and all-loving God, who purely out of goodness and mercy had revealed Himself to humankind.

In Berlin, Dietrich Bonhoeffer had little contact with Barth. He did not even read him at any length. Yet there is little doubt that the teachings of Karl Barth were finding a ready home in the budding conscience of Dietrich Bonhoeffer. In fact, one of the early papers Dietrich wrote for Seeberg came back marked with red exclamation points and had "Nein" scribbled all over it because, in the professor's opinion, it showed too much Barthian influence.

Dietrich's three-and-a-half years at the university were as much a pleasure as a chore. He was constantly busy. Yet the family creed insisted one should never play the martyr or even talk too much about school, except with other students. During this time, Dietrich didn't let up on his outings to the Baltic, to the summerhouse, to Switzerland and Italy, or to plays, operas, and readings.

During the university years, Dietrich also fell mildly—and briefly—in love. Although he had watched a whole family of brothers and sisters choose mates, for Dietrich the world of romantic love was new and strange. Nothing ever came of the relationship, and the two families downplayed it, during and afterward, though the halfhearted affection lasted for years. The girl was a distant cousin, and the feelings were considerably cooled by Dietrich's year in Barcelona. His brothers predicted he would never marry, and they were proved right.

The Evangelical Church expected theological students to gain practical experience in addition to their theoretical knowledge. Dietrich was rather green at the whole idea of running a parish. The only time he had ever been around one was for an occasional wedding or the performance of *St. Matthew's Passion*. He promptly got his feet wet as the understudy of Pastor Karl Meumann in Grunewald, where Dietrich took over the children's worship and instruction. On Friday nights, he gathered his staff of teachers and gave them the background they would need to teach the youngsters their Sunday lessons. On Sundays he helped with the main service and taught a confirmation class. Among those he recruited as helpers was his sister Susanne.

Dietrich was a considerable success with the young people, but he did have one problem. Too many children were leaving their own classes to join the one taught by Dietrich. What to do? He didn't want to bother Meumann. The problem sounded rather boastful. So he wrote to a slightly older acquaintance, now graduated, a man out in the ministry.

Meanwhile a new youth group developed out of the Sunday school, which Dietrich called the Thursday Group. Most members were boys beyond confirmation age who were trying to make their way in the world. Sometimes they held discussions at Dietrich's home on Wangenheimstrasse. Sometimes they talked en route to a play or to the beach. In a sense, he was running a mini-university, with discussions on a variety of subjects: religion, culture, politics, literature. Many of these youngsters continued to write to him when he moved to Barcelona and, later, to New York.

In conducting services at Grunewald, Dietrich tried to make worship lively, even if he had to stray from the biblical text. Some of the young people jokingly accused him of combining the Bible with Old Norse sagas. During Advent, he talked of an old woman caught in a blizzard at a woodcutter's hut with the door locked from the inside. She could not open the door. Only someone who was inside could open it—God. Another of his stories was about mushrooms in the forest and how the devil stole a pot of paint and turned them into attractive baubles. Unpainted, natural, they made a good meal, but larded with paint, they were of no use to anyone.

For his doctoral thesis, Bonhoeffer chose the title *Sanctorum Communio*, the communion of saints. For a young man of 21, it was a remarkable piece of scholarship, though the language was somewhat florid and overblown. In almost 300 pages, worked out in great detail over a period of 18 months, Dietrich had tried to paint an elaborate vision of what the church should be. His view of the church and its place in the world was not wholly acceptable either to the liberals, who saw in it too much of Barth, or to the Barthians, who saw in it too much sociology. He tried to say with St. Paul that those who believed really *were* the church, not *ought to be* the church. What they believed flowed directly from their relationship to Christ. The thesis caused a considerable stir, both

53

for what it said and because it had been written by one so young. Just before Christmas 1927, Bonhoeffer defended his thesis, receiving his degree with the highest honors, *summa cum laude*.

For the holidays, the whole family, including a growing brood of grandchildren, trooped to the home on Wangenheim-strasse. For the first time since Walter's death, Dr. Bonhoeffer again kept the family chronicle. In January, Dietrich preached his farewell sermon at Grunewald, obviously moved when the pastor prayed for him at the altar and when the children's choir sang him their good-byes.

8

Barcelona

At the age of 22, Dietrich left home for a year to become assistant pastor of a German congregation in Barcelona. Never before had he really been separated from his family. At Tübingen there had been a sister and a grandmother. And in Rome, his brother had been with him most of the time. Now Dietrich was on his own, learning what it meant to be a pastor. Compared to most 22-year-olds, he was still an emotional fledgling, an individual with great gifts of intellect and personality but who was inwardly insecure.

The vicarate had been arranged from Berlin. Like most Germans, Dietrich was fascinated by the lands of the Mediterranean. He looked forward to Spain with considerable excitement. He was not disappointed. The snow of Berlin gave way to rain in Paris, and when the train pulled into the station in Barcelona on February 15, 1928, he was greeted by the sight of blossoming almonds.

The drastic change was not only one of climate, but one of people and culture. For the first time in his life, Dietrich realized how narrow a social stratum he had come from: upper-class, aristocratic, academic. He took a room in a pension run by two German widows. Klaus later described it as primitive and Spartan, sunny yet airy. The shared bath at the end of the hall was not as modern as that of a German third-class railroad carriage—a drastic change for a young man who had grown up in a mansion with a half dozen spotless bathrooms.

As a seaport and as capital of Catalonia, Barcelona was as great a trade center as Madrid. The congregation Dietrich helped serve had a distinct personality. His parishioners were mostly businessmen, along with families from the diplomatic colony, retired widows, teachers who had fled south for the sun, ex-sailors who had jumped ship, even eccentric lion tamers, acrobats, or dancers who had dropped out from the Krone Circus when it toured Spain.

Pastor Fritz Olbricht was a kindly man who welcomed his new assistant with enthusiasm. The older pastor had grown a little set in his ways, more like an easygoing Spaniard than a German. Yet he still showed some concern for his flock. The heaviest cross Pastor Olbricht had to bear every year was arranging his vacation. No one else was available to fill the pulpit. The real reason he wanted Dietrich was so he could take a three-month holiday to visit his relatives in Germany.

For decades, the German church had worried about how it should care for its countrymen abroad, especially those who lived in Latin countries. Where the German colonists were numerous enough, the *Aussenamt*, a kind of foreign affairs office of the Evangelical Church, established regular parishes, sending out clergymen from the homeland. Such congregations flourished in Rome, Florence, Paris, and Barcelona, as well as in Buenos Aires, Rio de Janeiro, Asuncion, and Santiago.

The colony in Barcelona counted about 6,000 souls, even if normal church attendance numbered only about 40. After Dietrich arrived, the attendance doubled, then doubled again. At first Pastor Olbricht announced the preaching schedule, but when the crowds for Bonhoeffer's sermons grew much greater than those for his own, the announcements stopped.

Within the Evangelical Church, there was a mixture of Lutheran and Reformed. There were somewhat more Reformed brethren in the parish at Barcelona. Its controlling body was not a church council, as Lutherans knew, but a presbytery. In fact, when Dietrich wrote to his grandmother about his situation, she did not even know what a presbytery was because she had been raised in the isolation of Lutheran orthodoxy among the old Junker families of East Prussia.

Dietrich's first impressions of his parish were mixed. He missed the intellectual life of Berlin. The young people he met in

Spain all planned to enter the family business and not study at a university. He was no longer getting the latest books and journals. He had hoped to keep track of what was going on in the world outside the parish. Back home, the democratic regime of Gustav Stresemann was making Germany more stable and independent, though there already were signs of the depression that was soon to come. Even in volatile Spain, the government seemed stable. Ever since Roman days, Catalonia had enjoyed a high standard of living compared with the arid plateaus of Aragon and Castile. Yet in another five years, Spain was to split apart in a bloody civil war.

To some degree, the German church in Barcelona had adopted the Spanish lifestyle. This congregation did not really need two pastors, but having two certainly made life more pleasant. Dietrich also received a tremendous welcome from his "bishop." Although there were no congregations in Madrid or Majorca, there were small colonies of Germans there. Dietrich delighted in making visits, holding services, and offering Communion in private homes, perhaps baptizing a newborn or instructing a confirmand.

To one so hooked on cleanliness and sanitation, the old Gothic quarter was shocking—a squalid medieval relic where rotting oranges and potatoes were scrounged from the cobblestones to keep some urchin from starving. Dietrich thought Barcelona the dirtiest city he had ever seen. In contrast, the *barrio gotico,* the old Gothic quarter, also boasted beneath its streets magnificent Roman mosaics and Greek amphorae. In the same area was the medieval palace where Ferdinand and Isabella had welcomed home a jubilant Christopher Columbus, who brought with him American Indians, parrots, and a lizard-like iguana that was bigger than a man.

Dietrich's wanderings in Barcelona were not restricted to the older quarters. On the western rim of the city rose Tibidabo, a beautiful Spanish blend of mountain, amusement park, and shrine. He reached this on a creaky cog railway. The mountain took its name from the Latin words *tibi dabo,* recalling the peak from which the devil had shown Christ the world and said, "This will I give you." In the heat of summer, half the town lounged in the cool air of the mountaintop, where on a clear day one could see Minorca.

Like Ernest Hemingway, who was roaming Spain about the same time, Dietrich became an aficionado of bullfighting. When Klaus came for Easter, he accused his brother of preaching short sermons to get to the *plaza de toros* in time. In a letter to Sabine, Dietrich tried to describe his fascination with bullfighting. He compared it to man's primitive struggle for survival, an emotional outlet that helped the Spanish people work out their aggression. He even drew theological meaning from the bullring. First, the crowd cheered the bull, which was snorting, prancing, and charging. A few minutes later, they cheered the *torero*, especially when he made a dangerous pass or showed unusual poise. This quick switch of allegiance Dietrich likened to that of the crowd that had welcomed Christ into Jerusalem. On Palm Sunday, they screamed "Hosanna," but on Good Friday, they shouted, "Crucify Him!"

With Klaus or with his parents, Dietrich toured Toledo, Cordoba, Seville, Madrid, Majorca, and Algeciras. With his parents, he wandered as far afield as France, visiting Nimes, Arles, and Avignon. With Klaus, there was an excursion into Morocco on the ferry across the Straits of Gibraltar. He and Klaus were still determined to learn something of Arab life, this time without alienating their hosts, as they had done in Libya.

In Madrid, they bought a painting that purported to be a Picasso. It did have the right colors and surrealist flair. Back in Berlin, Klaus turned down an offer of 5,000 marks for it. With a photograph, he inquired of Picasso whether the painting was an original. Picasso would say only that there were several artists in Madrid good enough to turn out perfect copies, and from a photo he could never be sure.

Dietrich tried to practice the native lifestyle. He enjoyed an occasional evening at the bar, sipping sherry, swallowing raw oysters, nibbling artichokes. He read *Don Quixote* in the original. With boys from the church, he played not soccer, but *belote*. He visited Catholic shrines. He enjoyed the colorful processions of Corpus Christi. Dietrich sought out miracle plays that featured an age-old aspect of Iberia: a debate, or *tenso,* between the divines of Christianity and those of Islam, which dated to the time of the Muslim conquest of Spain.

Dietrich quickly became a part of the community. He played the piano for the German choral society. He joined the tennis club. He took an active part in the *Deutscher Hilfsverein*, a charitable group that provided food, lodging, and cash to down-and-out Germans. He was rather shocked to find himself so naive, believing nearly all the hard luck stories he heard, then discovering later they were only half true. The world of the poor and the homeless was enlightening, a side of life he had never before experienced.

He wanted to broaden his theological horizons, yet Dietrich found Spanish Catholicism dull and hidebound in comparison to German or Italian practices. Then he had a brainstorm. He would go to India. He would study the sutras of Buddhism. He would merge the central themes of the Reformation, now rediscovered by Karl Barth, with those of the East. He would study in the ashrams of Mahatma Gandhi, that great Indian who had practiced passive resistance.

Dietrich thought the venture not in the least impractical. He failed to consider how Gandhi might receive an unknown young theologian, let alone a 22-year-old of the upper bourgeoisie who felt ill at ease when a Western bathroom was not spotless or when the bedsheets did not smell of lavender. Dietrich excitedly wrote his grandmother at Tübingen, and by return mail came a check for expenses. He set up a separate bank account. For more than a decade, Dietrich was to dream of India.

Meanwhile, Dietrich worked his way into the hearts of his parishioners. At first some had laughed at his northern ways. He wore a fashionable hat, a bowler. In Berlin this was high style. Along the shores of the Costa Brava, however, any hat marked him as a foreigner. He made his deepest impression on the young, just as he had done at Grunewald. He immediately started a Sunday school but had only one pupil. That did not daunt him. Talking at the German school, visiting every home, chatting with the youngsters themselves, he quickly gathered a group of 40. Soon he also collected a separate band of schoolboys, usually meeting in the sitting room of the home where he boarded. He was good for them and they for him, talking of careers, of church, of politics. They put on a special Christmas party for him, afraid he might be homesick. Although always careful to hide his charity, he bought one of the poorer boys a bicycle and another a camping tent.

Dietrich was rather surprised to see these children had all become half Spanish. Was this the climate, the school system, or simply an attitude of *dolce far niente*, of sitting in the sun and taking life easy? A little shocked at their religious ignorance, he suggested he teach a course in religion at the German school. This the presbyters scotched. They did not want to raise difficulties with the Spanish church, and they also thought Pastor Olbricht would not want to carry on after Dietrich left.

Barcelona was a good city for culture. The music, the plays, the opera, the painting were far better than Dietrich expected. He became especially fond of El Greco's work. He often went to Toledo to visit the painter's villa, where precious canvases were hung along roofed porticoes open to the air. For the rest of his life, Dietrich sought out other El Grecos in New York, Washington, London, and Berlin.

The diary that he boldly began when he first arrived was soon abandoned. Mornings, afternoons, evenings—Dietrich was almost never at home. He had brought along a copy of his doctoral thesis, *The Communion of Saints*. His hope had been to simplify it for the ordinary reader. Yet he much preferred to wander among the sunny stalls of the *Ramblas*, bright with cages of singing birds, or to lounge beneath the statue of Christopher Columbus that guarded the harbor. For the first time, Dietrich learned to relax, to take life less seriously. Yet he also felt a tinge of guilt about his "laziness."

In Barcelona he also learned the art of preaching. In Berlin sermonizing had proved difficult. He had found it almost impossible to translate the Gospel from the language of a scholar into that of the marketplace. His audience at the church in Barcelona was a real challenge, knowledgeable and worldly-wise but without much understanding of theology. Dietrich may well have preached more sermons in his one year at Barcelona than in any other five years of his life. Still inexperienced in the pulpit, he often spent a whole week writing word for word what he wanted to say. Many of the sermons of those days still exist. They usually begin with a clever device to catch the listener's ear. In one he describes the ark of the covenant and what it meant to the people of Israel. As they carried it through the desert and across the Jordan, they came to love and appreciate it. It represented the power and the glory of God. Dietrich said Christ was like the ark of the covenant. Anyone who knew Him was forever captivated by God's power and glory.

More and more Dietrich began to preach like Karl Barth. Both could write fairly simple sermons, no matter how difficult and obscure their topics. Dietrich also delivered a series of lectures about religion and its place in the modern world. These were well attended by the people of the parish. They were also the first draft for his book *The Cost of Discipleship*.

During the Advent season, the presbytery suddenly realized that the year of Dietrich's contract was nearing an end. They could not bear to see him go. He had enlivened the church and ingratiated himself with the young people. They encouraged him to stay, but Dietrich had to turn them down. For one thing, he was not yet ordained. And after a year in the pastorate, he now wanted to try his hand at teaching. To accomplish this, he first had to pass the "habilitation," the post-doctoral dissertation required before one could teach at the university.

Before he left, however, Dietrich bought a souvenir as impressive as the "Picasso" that Klaus had carted home. For Dietrich it was a huge brazier made of carved chestnut with a brass bowl big enough to barbecue a sheep. It made a spectacular trophy for the parlor in Berlin, and it later accompanied him to the seminary at Finkenwalde.

Dietrich Bonhoeffer left Barcelona in February 1929 and headed home to a snow-covered Grunewald. But the memories of Spain lingered. His friends continued to visit and write. A year later, just before his trip to New York, Dietrich sandwiched in a delightful excursion to Barcelona, reveling in the magic taste of coffee on the terraces of Mount Tibidabo, shouting *ole* at the *plaza de toros,* and paying homage at Montserrat to the mystical black statue of the Virgin, the *moroneta.*

9

Return to Berlin

Even now Berlin is a city of lakes and pines, of the River Spree and the Wannsee, pastoral except for the colorful sails and the weekend boaters. In Bonhoeffer's day, the western suburbs were even more country-like; every house seemed a private estate.

To leave the pink blossoms of the almonds in Barcelona and return to the snowdrifts of Berlin was not ideal timing, but Dietrich was in a hurry. He was turning 24. He wanted to finish his habilitation as quickly as he could in hopes of becoming a professor. By church regulation, he could not be ordained until he was 25. That was a built-in safeguard against youthful enthusiasm and immaturity. He also nursed hopes for further travel, to America, perhaps, and the Far East.

The Berlin Dietrich had known was undergoing rapid change, both politically and academically. Older Germans recalled the glories they knew before World War I, and younger ones were shouting for revolution. The Depression aggravated all this turmoil, and when Chancellor Stresemann died in the fall of 1929, just before the Great Crash in the United States, the Weimar Republic lost whatever stability it had established.

Young people wanted a quick solution. On the left, the Communists fought for power, and on the right, it was the National Socialists, the Nazis. The largest party of the middle, the Conservatives, lost strength almost daily. Dietrich was not too interested in the practical side of politics at this stage of his life, though his brothers Karl-Friedrich and Klaus and his brothers-in-law Rüdiger Schleicher, Hans von Dohnanyi, and Gerhard Leibholz talked of little else.

The big estate on Wangenheimstrasse had now almost emptied. Except for Dietrich, all the children had married and gone out into the world. Susanne, the youngest of the family, chose Pastor Walter Dress as a husband. The oldest, Karl-Friedrich, married Greta von Dohnanyi, daughter of the Hungarian composer and sister of Hans. Klaus, three years older than Dietrich, married Emmi Delbruck.

Dietrich wrote excellent birthday letters, poems, and telegrams, and was a popular godfather in a family that was regularly producing offspring. He became especially fond of Walter Dress. Walter was not only a good theologian, but a first-class botanist and Dietrich's constant companion in the woods around Grunewald. The cousin with whom Dietrich so enjoyed Friedrichsbrunn, Hans Christoph von Hase, had switched his studies from physics to theology after his exposure to Karl Barth. Now the cousins became even closer friends.

The oddest and strongest relationship, the only one that brought Dietrich out of his shell, was with Franz Hildebrandt. These two met just before Dietrich defended his thesis and left for Spain. They had argued through half the night. Franz was an ardent socialist, of the non-Nazi sort, son of an art historian and a Jewish mother. The friend-antagonist relationship between Franz and Dietrich bloomed again after the return from Barcelona when they happened to meet at a presentation of *St. Matthew's Passion*. Hildebrandt was a loyal disciple of von Harnack and often characterized Bonhoeffer as a Barthian. They continued to see each other and go places together. It was Franz who persuaded Dietrich to hear von Harnack's exciting sermons on Christian socialism in the pulpit at Berlin Moabit. That was when Dietrich confessed there were only two preachers in all Berlin to whom he could listen.

Hildebrandt accused Bonhoeffer of being a biblicist, of depending too much on the Bible and on Luther, of discarding reason. Yet when Dietrich won his lectorship, Franz presented him with a book of quotations from Luther inscribed: "To my old enemy on the occasion of his habilitation." The two talked of taking over a working man's parish in East Berlin, with Bonhoeffer as the senior pastor and Hildebrandt as the assistant, preaching all sides of political and theological questions.

During the year Bonhoeffer was in Barcelona, there had been drastic changes in the theological faculty at the University of Berlin. Dietrich had maintained solid contact with his mentor, Seeberg, who had retired and whose post had been filled by Wilhelm Lütgert. The assistantship, which Dietrich had hoped would fall vacant, did not. But Lütgert found him an assistant lectureship, a position that for the time being was unsalaried but that would allow Dietrich to complete his habilitation. The work was not glamorous: assisting with the seminar, reading the papers, recommending the books, stocking the shelves, unlocking the doors, even cleaning the blackboard. The work kept Dietrich busy but not happy. He did appreciate one fringe benefit. The assignment excused him from attending the evening sessions for ordinands. He did not really want to know too much about the practical problems of running a parish and felt himself superior to the other candidates.

For habilitation, Dietrich needed another thesis. This one bore the title *Act and Being*. Focusing on the church and its place in the world, it was a deeper development of the *Communio Sanctorum*. Dietrich was still having difficulty getting *The Communion of Saints* into print. Completed nearly two years earlier, now rewritten and simplified, he sent it fruitlessly from printer to printer. Despite encouraging recommendations from Seeberg, Dietrich felt frustrated and unfulfilled. Finally the firm of Trowitzsch made an offer, though with a catch. Dietrich would have to pay 1,000 marks toward the typesetting and binding. Even then the publisher showed little enthusiasm; there were scores of theologians begging to have their doctoral dissertations printed. Dietrich agreed to the printers' terms, though the manuscript did not appear until after he had left for America. Few copies went to reviewers and only a few to friends. The bill went to his parents. It was considerably more than he had bargained for. Actually the book suffered a quiet death before it was ever born, scarcely noticed by anyone. Dietrich himself later regarded it as a kind of youthful but disappointing exercise.

Act and Being, his second book, frustrated Dietrich even more than the first. He wrote it for learned specialists, not for ordinary lay readers. It tackled the views of many of his older contemporaries, for example, Barth, Heidegger, Bultmann, and Tillich. He finished the work in 12 months, in February 1930, as the thesis for his habilitation. This book also bombed. Despite strong support from Lütgert and Paul Althaus, the printing firm of Bertelsmann asked him for 200 marks to help pay for publication. At least the price of publishing his books was coming down, if that was any mark of success. Dietrich wondered if he would ever be a successful theologian or writer.

Besides the thesis, Dietrich also was required to present a public lecture: "The Question of Man in Contemporary Philosophy and Theology." Dietrich's speaking style was far livelier than his writing. The mere appearance at the podium of a 24-year-old with a mop of tawny hair, in rimless glasses, still too young to be ordained, won him considerable plaudits among the Berlin theologians.

Dietrich did not let the months of his habilitation become a grind, even if he was eager to finish the requirements. He was already laying plans for a year of study in America. He read the best novels and saw the best plays, taking special delight in the religious novels of Georges Bernanos. He developed many new friendships, now that his married brothers and sisters had scattered across Germany.

Dietrich, as a longtime friend and neighbor of Adolf von Harnack, was asked to speak at the professor's memorial service, though he had declined to write a thesis under the grand old scholar. The affair was held at Harnack House in Goethe Hall. Other speakers honoring the 87-year-old professor included the most influential men of Germany: the Minister of State, the Minister of Culture, the Minister of the Interior, and the Director of the National Library. Dietrich represented the student body, recalling the many friendly discussions the two had had on the U-bahn. He spoke so effectively, even in comparison to the highest dignitaries of state, that those who formerly thought Dietrich a little argumentative and brash now saw him in a new and friendlier light.

10

Discovering America

Right from the start, Dietrich Bonhoeffer had reservations about going to school in the United States. In his opinion, American seminaries were little more than trade schools for preachers. Sensing his hesitation, Karl-Friedrich suggested he might not want to go as a student at all, but wait a few years and go as a lecturer.

Still, Dietrich was not yet 25, too young for ordination or a lectureship. The travel in Spain and Italy had more than whetted his appetite for other cultures and new insights. He was restless. A disciple of Karl Barth, though he had never met the man, he realized he would face considerable hostility in the United States. Highly trained systematic and dogmatic theologians from Europe were not all that welcome in a church atmosphere that stressed the social gospel, which insisted on action rather than thought.

The question of where to study was solved when Dietrich was offered a Sloane Fellowship at Union Theological Seminary in New York, a school with strong ties to Columbia University. If he was going for culture rather than theology, what he feared most was landing in the hinterlands, away from a big city. He disliked the places popular with other German theologues: Princeton, Harvard, Yale. He thought them too strongly influenced either by the social gospel or by 17th-century orthodoxy. Yet any of these could have offered him more of his beloved systematics and dogmatics, more Greek and Hebrew, than Union.

Dietrich's cabin companion aboard ship was an American missionary, Dr. Lucas, president of a college at Lahore, Pakistan. Lucas genuinely excited him about Buddhism and what it could teach a Western theologian. He offered his hospitality if Dietrich should ever make it to India. Long into the night, the two discussed the politics of Mahatma Gandhi, that seer who knew enough about British sensibilities to gamble that no British engineer would ever drive a locomotive through a trackful of beggars. Once in New York, Dietrich immediately made the rounds of the travel agencies, exploring passage to India. His sisters had suggested he ask his parents for a loan if he really wanted to go to India, and his still sympathetic grandmother encouraged him never to give up. He discovered, however, that a trip to New Delhi from New York was more difficult than one from Berlin—longer, costlier, more indirect. For the time being, he would concentrate on the New World.

His introduction to Union Seminary was not altogether satisfying, to judge from Dietrich's letters home. Before leaving Berlin, he had put together a list of American idioms and also one of arguments against Germany's war guilt. Unlike the two other European students that year, he did not register for a master's degree, as his fellowship stipulated. An American master's degree was beneath the dignity of one who held a doctorate from Berlin. His student visa forced him to attend classes, but he considered the lectures simplistic and naïve.

Life in a dormitory was difficult as well. At home he had been sheltered. Now, somewhat surprised, somewhat miffed, he wrote home about the students' "endless friendliness" and "the thousandfold hello." He was annoyed by those who barged into his room without knocking, though in time he came to appreciate their openness and genuineness.

The faculty boasted some practical scholars, even if they were not oriented to the fashions of German theology. They included Reinhold Niebuhr, John Baillie, James Moffatt, and Harry Emerson Fosdick. What Union really stressed was a practical involvement with society. That was what Walter Rauschenbusch had once proclaimed the "Social Gospel." At first Dietrich was somewhat shocked by Union. He could find little of theology: no systematics, no dogmatics, not even much history. When he quoted Luther, he was laughed at. Barthianism was unknown, even to the faculty.

Nevertheless, Dietrich soon became a friendly and happy member of the community. The social freedom between student and professor reflected none of the stiffness he had known in Europe, and between students there was no reserve at all. What endeared him to the others at Union was his forthrightness and his delightful sense of humor. Paul Lehmann, a graduate assistant, once told how Dietrich declined an invitation to play tennis on the grounds that a match between an expert like Dietrich and an amateur like Paul would hurt their friendship rather than help it.

Although the classroom was disappointing, what fascinated Dietrich was America itself. In that sense, perhaps, he was fortunate not to be at Princeton or Yale. He examined every aspect of church and society. He visited soup kitchens, settlement houses, YMCAs, prisons, stock exchanges, playgrounds, courtrooms, political meetings, hospitals, and asylums. He had constant invitations to speak. His English blossomed quickly under this challenge. He made the rounds of pulpits, classrooms, mission societies, and ladies' auxiliaries. Distinctive and handsome, he became something of a social lion, not just for his dinner conversation, but for his performances at the piano.

Now in his mid-20s, Dietrich, for the first time in his life, began to make deep and long-lasting friendships. One of his new friends was an African American student from Harlem, Frank Fisher. Slenderly built with attractive features, Frank was buoyant and stable. As a member of the Abyssinian Baptist Church, deep in the heart of the ghetto, Frank involved Dietrich more and more in African American culture. For a time, Dietrich missed no opportunity to visit Harlem, to teach Sunday school and Bible class, to share in potlucks, to eat soul food, and to explore the northern half of Manhattan. Later, Frank introduced Dietrich to the Philadelphia ghetto and showed him around Howard University in Washington, D.C. Together, they attended a conference of the National Council of Churches. When Frank was refused seating at a restaurant, Dietrich promptly walked out too.

Another close companion was Paul Lehmann. At Paul's apartment, Dietrich celebrated his 25th birthday. He wrote Sabine that they could not even drink her health in Rhine wine because

America was in the middle of Prohibition. All alcohol was prohibited, except for Holy Communion or for medicinal purposes.

Two fellow Europeans also held fellowships at Union the same year. Erwin Sutz, a Swiss, adapted magically to America. He and Dietrich were both gifted pianists, and in that alone they had much in common. Together, they made the rounds of New York's musical attractions: operas, symphonies, and ballets. Sutz sang with a choral society and several times performed at Carnegie Hall. The other European was Jean Lasserre, a Frenchman. Although at first this relationship was not as warm as the one with Sutz, Dietrich and Lasserre maintained the bond of friendship throughout their lives. Lasserre was an outspoken pacifist who did a good job of convincing most of his classmates that Jesus' words, "Blessed are the peacemakers," really ought to be taken as gospel truth. Already in Germany, Dietrich had shown an interest in pacifism, which is one reason he admired the Buddhists. Now Lasserre stirred his inclinations even more. Lasserre also planted the seeds that later grew into Dietrich's most famous book, *The Cost of Discipleship*. In that book, Dietrich referred to Lasserre as a "living saint."

During his year in New York, Dietrich worked hard to maintain his ties to Germany. His classmates marveled at his energies. Sutz accused him of supporting the telephone and telegraph companies all by himself. Seldom did a day go by when he was not in contact with his family by letter, phone, or telegram. He was lonely, still tied tightly to the shelter of home. He carried on a detailed correspondence with Karl-Friedrich, who also had spent a year in America, mainly about the problems of the African Americans. Dietrich came to know these problems well from his connections in Harlem, as well as through his visits to Philadelphia and Washington. Karl-Friedrich agreed the race problem was serious, perhaps as bad as the question of the Jews in Germany.

Dietrich's father was his political interpreter, along with the newspapers, regarding events in Germany. Repeatedly, Dietrich wrote for more detail, for clarification. Much was going on that year: the posting of Nazi flags, disturbances at the universities, troubles in the churches, political scandals, and anti-Jewish demonstrations. During the year Dietrich was in New York, the number of Nazis in the Reichstag jumped from 12 to 107, though in far-off America these developments did not seem important.

Vacations proved a delight for so seasoned a traveler. At Thanksgiving Dietrich headed to Philadelphia and Washington, not just for the travel and music and theology, but to get acquainted with the American branch of his grandmother's family, the Tafels. Christmas was more special. With Erwin Sutz, he accepted an invitation to preach to the German colony in Cuba. Katie Horn, the companion and governess of his childhood, now taught at the German school in Havana. Dietrich's sermon was not so much focused on Christmas as on the problems of the new year. He spoke of a worried Moses standing atop Mount Nebo, wondering what really awaited the people of Israel as they prepared to enter the Promised Land.

By May, Dietrich had given up any hope of going home the long way, through India. Yet he did not give up plans to see more of the United States, along with a good chunk of Mexico. Perhaps worried by what they might have heard about its morals and nightlife, Dietrich's parents wrote and suggested he avoid New Orleans.

Meanwhile, Dietrich was cooking up a trip with Paul Lehmann, Erwin Sutz, and Jean Lasserre. The young foreigners were offered the loan of a dying Oldsmobile, and Dietrich set about applying for a driver's license. Whether his failure was really the fault of the car, no one will ever know. Sutz admitted the wheels did not always turn in prompt obedience to the steering wheel. Lehmann said Dietrich was turned down by examiners at least three or four times. Dietrich said he failed because he refused to offer a bribe. In any case, the four set out, licensed or not, dropping Lehmann at Chicago and Sutz at St. Louis. Lasserre had friends in Mexico City who had promised food and sightseeing. Steering a safe course around New Orleans (though the dangers would be greater at Matamoros or Tampico), the two travelers got the creaky Oldsmobile as far as the Texas border. The advice of the mechanics they consulted was to abandon it, even burn it. Instead, the two left it for repairs and traveled 1,500 miles into Mexico by train.

At Victoria Teachers College in Mexico City, the two Europeans lectured on peace. Those who heard them thought it odd that a Frenchman and a German should be such good friends because the two countries were so much at odds. Apparently, the pyramids and temples of the Toltecs proved more exciting than the theologues had expected. Vastly moved, absorbing the whole story of human sacrifice and bloody conquest, Dietrich for once was too busy to write long letters home.

The time in Mexico passed all too quickly. At the Texas border, Bonhoeffer and Lasserre had troubles coming in from Mexico with only their student visas. With no reentry permits, they were detained. Only telegrams from the German ambassador and from Paul Lehmann helped prove who they were and that they really did have boat tickets from New York.

On the long journey across the American heartland, Dietrich had time to rethink his year in the states. He was troubled by what he had seen of America, both its politics and its religion. There was too much interest in feeding the poor, in clothing the naked, in holding church socials and card parties. Yet he admired the loyalty the people had for their churches, something rare in the state churches of Europe.

What Europe needed, he thought, was some of the American dedication and what America needed was a clearer insight into the whole purpose of the church. They were strange bedfellows, Europe and America—politically, religiously, and socially. But perhaps they were no stranger than a German aristocrat and a French pacifist driving a ramshackle Oldsmobile across America with no driver's license.

11

Troubled Times

The Dietrich Bonhoeffer who came home to Berlin in the summer of 1931 expected a bright future. He was only 25, already licensed to teach at the university, and ready to be ordained. He had just finished a year of study in New York and still cherished the happy memories of a similar one in Barcelona. Yet he was not altogether happy. He had never been able to plow a straight furrow, but he had taken things as they came—switching his enrollment from Tübingen to Berlin, running off to Italy and Spain and America, hesitating between a church and a classroom.

Dietrich had not even been able to fall in love. Somehow he was different from others, even his brothers and sisters—too dependent on his mother, too protected, too gifted, too hesitant to set permanent goals. In one of his sermons, he described himself when he talked about the Old Testament figure Jacob, a stranger to his own country and even to himself. Before crossing the last stream into the Promised Land, Jacob struggled all night with an angel. The struggle seemed never to end, like a bad dream. Dietrich sometimes felt his own life was something of a wrestling match with a nightmarish angel, one against which he was always struggling but never winning.

The next two years were crowded with challenges and successes, but they were also times of frustration and disappointment. With the Depression knocking Germany to her knees, the rapid rise of the Nazis, and serious disturbances in the church,

Dietrich's dreams for success met many unexpected roadblocks. A dozen other men might have relished being in his boots, especially his youth work for the World Alliance of Churches and the travel this provided—to St. Leonard's and Cambridge and Epsom in England, to Geneva and Gland in Switzerland, to Westerburg in Germany, to Ciernohorske Kupele in Czechoslovakia, and to Sofia in Bulgaria.

Scarcely had he paid his respects to the big old house on Wangenheimstrasse than Dietrich left to seek out Karl Barth at the University of Bonn. From New York, his Swiss friend Sutz had written a letter of introduction, and Dietrich was quick to follow it up. Although Bonhoeffer had earned the rank of *privatdozent*, or private instructor, was a licensed lecturer, and had published two books, his name was wholly unknown to Barth. Nevertheless, the 45-year-old Swiss pastor, who had suddenly become the star of German theology, quickly learned to admire the 25-year-old disciple who for three weeks joined his seminar and, unlike most of his students, always could find an apt quotation from Luther or Augustine.

To Dietrich, the pipe-smoking Barth was highly impressive. Not one bit pompous or dogmatic, Barth showed a dedication both to faith and to reason that was unmatched by any other theological professor Dietrich had encountered. Their walks, their chats, their meals together—this was the kind of warmth herr doktor professors seldom practiced, even with interesting *privatdozents*. Although Barth would eventually flee to his native Switzerland, Dietrich remained a lifelong admirer and correspondent.

Back in Berlin, the classroom success Dietrich might have anticipated was hampered by the Depression. The university was still riding the crest of past glory, with nearly 1,000 theology students. Yet there was scarcely money for professors already on the payroll and none for new ones. Under other circumstances, Dietrich might have considered a post outside Berlin at a smaller university. Because he was not yet ordained, however, he had to remain in his home district. Besides, his ties to his parents were strong, and he loved Berlin's music and opera. As a registered lecturer, he gave occasional lectures, but the only pay he received was the skimpy student fees. For a year and a half, Dietrich's life was a hodgepodge: delivering a periodic lecture, serving as student chaplain to the Technical University, teaching a confirmation class in one of Berlin's ghettos, or attending an ecumenical youth conference.

In many ways, Dietrich was frustrated. At 25 he was not yet considered mature enough to do the things he had always dreamed of, either in the classroom or in the parish. Even the troubled times seemed to work against him. Scarcely had he returned home when the government clamped a ban on foreign exchange. To travel outside Germany, he needed foreign currency, sometimes available at a discount of 15 percent, sometimes not available at all. He wrote Sutz and Lasserre they would now have to travel to Berlin because he could not go to Switzerland or France.

The hard times made the political crisis worse. Before 1930 the Nazi party had little influence either in the Reichstag or in the hearts of the people. The majority of Germans still supported the political parties of the center. This situation was beginning to change. In a three-year period, there were 400 deaths because of political riots or disturbances—usually the Nazis of the far right against the Communists of the far left. The courts consistently treated Nazi crimes against Communists with leniency, if any charges were brought at all.

Since the Treaty of Versailles, the German standard of living had fallen far below that of the French and the British, to whom the Germans were still paying large war reparations. During the height of the Depression, this brought on a new wave of nationalism. Fifteen years after the war, the Germans felt no need for economic dependence on France and England.

Dietrich was concerned about the political tensions he saw everywhere. Shortly after his return from New York, in the summer of 1931, he took part in a massive rally of Berlin clergymen. Later he wrote Sutz:

> The coming winter can hardly leave anyone in Germany unaffected. Seven million unemployed, that means fifteen or twenty million people hungry. I do not know how Germany or how the individual can survive this. Well-informed economists have told me we are rushing into a catastrophe no one can foresee or prevent. Can even the church survive such a catastrophe? Or will it be all over for all of us?

The Nazis were quick to capitalize on the unrest. They especially wanted the support of the church, and to a large degree, they succeeded in getting it. One of their favorite ploys was to don their brown shirts and attend services en masse. In a state church, where attendance was never good, the brown shirts often out-numbered the rest of the congregation. Dietrich was continually surprised to find that even 90 percent of the young theologians were pro-Nazi, wearing swastikas openly on their lapels.

For two years before the fateful Hitler takeover in 1933, the church leaders had mixed feelings about the Nazis. On both sides feelings ran high. Günther Dehn, dean of Magdeburg, was a strong anti-Nazi and pacifist. He commissioned a huge bronze statue by the expressionist sculptor Ernst Barlach and placed it in the cathedral, a sculpture that spoke loudly against war and mili-tarism. For this he became a marked man. When he was named professor at the University of Halle, the appointment caused a nationwide strike. No one who had been so vocal against a rearmed Germany ought to be appointed to anything, even street sweeper, the students argued. Later the same cathedral fell to the Nazis, who in turn removed the statue and filled the chancel with banners and flags.

Amid this turmoil, Bonhoeffer kept lecturing, going to youth conferences, preaching, and teaching confirmands. He was ordained as a clergyman of the Evangelical Church on November 15, 1931, but he does not seem to have considered the event a sig-nificant milestone. He knew none of the pastors who ordained him, either professionally or socially, and to his family the day was just another non-churchgoing Sunday. To him the day was significant not for the morning ordination, but for what hap-pened in the afternoon. Franz Hildebrandt, his friend and col-league, was then serving as an assistant pastor at Heilsbronnen and had arranged a special service for the hundredth anniversary of the death of G. W. F. Hegel, the illustrious German philosopher. To a dedicated Barthian like Bonhoeffer, who upgraded the impor-tance of faith and downgraded human learning, a service cele-brating the life of a skeptical philosopher like Hegel must have seemed strange indeed.

One pleasant project that Bonhoeffer and Hildebrandt worked on together was a new catechism. The impulse came from Hildebrandt. He claimed he couldn't find anything to interest the confirmation classes, thinking Luther's catechism too far out of date. So he came to Berlin, and he and Dietrich worked out an experimental one, brief and nontraditional. Bonhoeffer found the project exciting. Instead of using the standard elements, the creeds, the Ten Commandments, and the Lord's Prayer, Bonhoeffer and Hildebrandt focused on an informal credal statement attributed to Luther: "This is the Christian faith: to know what you should do and what has been handed on to you." The idea of trying to put the Gospel into modern language appealed so much to Dietrich that he continued to write creeds and catechisms all his life.

Dietrich was to need a confirmation guide of his own sooner than he expected. Shortly after his ordination, he was assigned as assistant at Zion Church in northern Berlin. The area was a working-class neighborhood, wholly unlike the rich western suburb of Grunewald where he had grown up. His salary was 400 marks. He took a room nearby because the commute from home would involve too much travel. Almost immediately he inherited what must have seemed the most unruly class of boys anywhere, far worse than those he had taught in Barcelona or Harlem. Even the way in which he met them tells something about the boys and their new teacher.

The school was an old, multistoried building with a central stairwell, and the aged pastor who was conducting him to the room for the first time warned Dietrich the boys would be hard to handle. The two preachers had scarcely reached the landing when they were pelted from above by orange peels and paper with a hullabaloo that was noisier than the Berlin Zoo. The older man lost his temper and started pushing and shoving to get the boys inside the classroom.

He tried to introduce Bonhoeffer to the students, and they immediately started chanting "Bon-Bon-Bon" at the top of their lungs. At least they stayed in the classroom. Dietrich quietly suggested the older pastor leave, and he leaned wordlessly against the blackboard, hands in pockets. There was no denying that he looked like an aristocrat, rimless gold glasses, signet ring with a family crest, tall, athletic, a mop of blond hair, blue eyes, nonchalant.

For five minutes the chatter continued. Bonhoeffer did not move. Then he began to talk at the level of a whisper. Those in front strained to hear. In a few minutes, curiosity won. The boys listened. He told a quick story or two about the African Americans in Harlem and asked if they wanted to hear more. They did. One boy obstinately unwrapped a sandwich and began eating. Bonhoeffer walked up to him, staring. The boy grew uncomfortable and wrapped up his sandwich. From then on, the confirmation class was Dietrich's.

There were about 50 boys in the group, and he made it a point to visit them all at home. When Dietrich preached at Zion, he used stories and examples to appeal to his class. With these 14-year-olds, Dietrich tried to develop a personal relationship. He instructed his landlady to give the boys access to his room, where he fed small groups of them a simple supper, played chess, and discussed books.

Because not every student owned a suit (and most could not afford one), Dietrich bought a bolt of woolen cloth and cut off lengths for each boy to make suits for their confirmation. After the service, he took them to the summerhouse at Friedrichsbrunn, with Pastor Bonhoeffer buying a group ticket. For many it was the first time they had left Berlin. His cousin Hans Christoph von Hase helped manage the outing. Not all the boys liked the mountains and the forests, but they certainly wolfed down the food and enjoyed kicking a soccer ball over the meadows.

Part of his control over the boys came from Dietrich's prowess as an athlete. He could swim circles around them. No one could begin to match him on the tennis court. Most of all, they idolized him for his genuineness. It was almost as if he were closer to them than to his own generation. Faithfully he visited them when they were sick or in trouble. He even bought one youngster a bicycle.

Bonhoeffer's lectures at the university started slowly. Only with the passage of several quarters did he begin to be noticed. In the usual German style, his students scuffled their shoes when the professor entered (the louder the noise, the more prestige a professor enjoyed). From Bonhoeffer's seminars, many during the evening, he gathered a loyal circle of disciples. Often these were students who had religious doubts, who, like Dietrich, had wondered about their faith. Many would follow him to the seminary at Finkenwalde. He was convinced he could teach them more outside the classroom than in, an insight he had gained from Karl Barth. Occasionally Dietrich gathered small groups for a weekend at a youth hostel.

When the Depression began to ease and the university finally received enough money to give Dietrich his back pay, he spent it buying a one-room shack in the woods at Biesenthal. There, the group talked theology long into the night, read books, swam, and hiked through the *Heide* (moor, or wasteland) and forest. Often they carted out food from the station at Stettin in a wheelbarrow: flour, potatoes, bacon, eggs. Bonhoeffer even brought some of his recordings of African American spirituals, always a favorite way for the students to spend an evening.

Actually the hut was so primitive, several students wondered how an aristocrat like Bonhoeffer could stand it. The only heat was a kerosene burner, which also served as the cookstove. The only furniture was a table and three decrepit bedsteads, certainly unlike anything at Wangenheimstrasse. Even in the summer, it was too damp for comfort, and it was almost never swept or dusted, except perhaps when some of the girls from the seminar came from a neighboring hostel.

Here more than anywhere else Dietrich's students came to know him. They were surprised at how much he knew about current novels and poems, about astronomy, and about psychiatry. They reveled in his stories about life in Harlem: the depth and sincerity of African American worship, its openness, its soul.

When the snows were too deep for travel to Biesenthal, Dietrich arranged a similar group in town. This met in the home of Wolf-Dieter Zimmermann at a huge old parsonage near the Königstor. Wolf's father was the church superintendent, and his son had the attic all to himself. There, a group of 12 or 15 gathered, just as in the woods, talking theology, arguing politics, smoking their Barthian pipes. In theory, the conversation in the attic was intended to be serious. The not-so-serious was saved for later in the evening at a Bierstube on the Alexanderplatz. The seminar grew so popular that it expanded to 50 or 60, which was in some ways unfortunate because they had to desert the cozy arrangements in Superintendent Zimmermann's attic for a regular classroom.

Despite the troubled times of the early 1930s, Dietrich was beginning to find himself—with young people, with fellow theologians, with the music and art and literature and theology that were all wrapped up in his personality. He was maturing, just in time for the difficult days that were ahead.

12

Ministry in Berlin

In addition to its burden of guilt and taxes, the Treaty of Versailles also caused problems in the Evangelical Church in Germany. To show their resistance, conservative churchgoers organized a faith movement. This movement stressed complete independence of the church from both the German government and the Allied Control Commission. It opposed contacts with churches outside the homeland. It even had some effect in Catholic circles, weakening ties with Rome. Basically, the faith movement grew from the concept of a "folk church," which had long been popular in Denmark and Norway, isolating the worship and faith of each nationality.

This was the obvious foundation for the "German Christians," later so effective in supporting Hitler. The movement tied faith to national pride. It said faith sprang from tradition, from soil, from homeland, and from bloodlines. It rejected anything of foreign origin. The Aryan race, supposedly Indo-European and without any Semitic blood, was to be the symbol of all that was best in Germany.

Later, Hitler climbed on this bandwagon with his devotion to Germany's prehistoric cultures. He was particularly fond of the Teutonic tribal gods, the Valkyrie and the Nibelungen that the operas of Richard Wagner had done so much to popularize. Hitler also made national shrines of the *hains*, the magic circles of stones in the forest where the clans had once worshiped.

Like Hansel and Gretel, the Evangelical Church was now lost in the woods and could not find the way out. Dietrich disliked the faith movement and preached against it. Other pastors argued that this weird combination of religion and nationalism would die a natural death and should not be needlessly publicized. For the most part, the people in the pews thought preachers should keep anything that bordered on politics out of the pulpit and stick to the truth of the Gospel.

Dietrich had been exposed to the same kind of religious nationalism when he was a parish pastor in Spain. Too many of his members thought of themselves first as Germans—with their clubs, tennis, soccer, and choral society—and only secondarily as Christians. Even the church was not so much a church, with strict religious goals, as an extension of German culture. Yet to be a good German, one at least had to belong to the German church.

Perhaps the pulpit was not the ideal place to combat the faith movement, but it was the only platform Dietrich had. Nearly a year before Hitler's rise to power, Dietrich had preached a ringing sermon on King Jehoshaphat, whose political naivete eventually forced him to return to Jehovah; after he had made so many mistakes, there was nowhere else to turn. The sermon cited the errors of present-day Christians, setting up nationalistic goals and asking God's help to achieve them:

> The prayers turn into programs, the requests into orders. ... Finally we append the name of God, so that He too is pressed into serving our tender plan, our scheming. ... This is what we enjoy listening to, and this is what we have listened to, for good or ill, a hundred times.

To some degree his friendships outside Germany alienated Dietrich from his own people. Within the Evangelical Church, there were many who felt they could look after their own theology without help from the outside. Dietrich did not mark himself out for popularity when he took part in a dozen youth conferences across Europe.

The sponsor for most of these meetings was the World Alliance for Promoting International Friendship through the Churches. Dietrich himself had strong reservations about the group. Sometimes he found it no more than a debating society, with no real roots in doctrine and faith. Committees such as "Life and Work" and "Faith and Order" seemed to him little more than tea-drinking societies of ecumenically minded clergymen who enjoyed escaping their parishes and offices. He annoyed his co-workers by continually pressing for a solid theological underpinning, not mere humanitarianism. If the purposes of the World Alliance were social justice and personal friendship rather than a fuller understanding of biblical faith, then for him the meetings were pointless.

Dietrich must have made a lasting impression on the ecumenicists. Wherever they gathered, the name of Bonhoeffer was brought up, whether for the novelty of his ideas or the depth of his insights. His square shoulders, sturdy build, and physical attractiveness did not hurt his popularity. Most of the conferees were in their 50s and 60s, not in their 20s. Also he was a trained theologian, fluent in English and French, a rarity among Germans. In addition, he had a sense of humor, an open enjoyment of life, and personal charm.

After he was named International Youth Secretary for northern Europe, one of four worldwide commissioners, the frequency of Dietrich's travel increased and the impact of his voice expanded. He was a natural interpreter of youth to many of the older churchmen, some of whom were beginning to lose touch with what was really happening in the world. That Dietrich did not really seem "German" and often criticized tendencies in his own church delighted the other ecumenicists, even as it alienated his fellow Germans.

At home in Berlin, Dietrich was now the assistant pastor at Zion Church, a massive relic of the Victorian Age. In the pulpit, he looked somewhat out of place, preaching to only 50 or 60 people in so huge a nave with perhaps only one or two people to each pew. His sermons were rather intellectual, with a large measure of politics thrown in, and he took delight in picking obscure texts from the Old Testament that no one else had ever chosen to preach on. Neighboring clergymen and Superintendent Zimmerman, though they liked him, thought him a little too political, a little too problematic.

In the classroom, Bonhoeffer's reputation continued to grow. The older, tenured members of the faculty, wrapped in their own affairs, showed little interest in anti-Nazi politics. Sometimes Dietrich suspected their hostility. He wrote Sutz that he felt like "a viper in their bosom." Nevertheless, he attracted a growing circle of students, not a little because he was politically oriented.

Sometime during 1931–32, Dietrich also shed his skin as a mere intellectual and became a practicing Christian. That had not yet been true in the autumn of 1931 at his ordination. When Paul Lehmann, the teaching assistant at Union, visited Dietrich in 1933, he noted a marked change. In New York, Dietrich had shown little interest in public worship, though he did not downgrade private prayer. Now Dietrich had begun to attend services almost every week, even when he was not conducting them. He set aside time for meditation and reading Scripture, not only as preparation for a lecture or sermon, but for his own growth. His students wondered if he might be taking the route of a pietist, about the worst insult they could think of for a Lutheran theologian. Increasingly he talked about the Sermon on the Mount, about feeding the hungry, clothing the naked, and visiting the imprisoned. Increasingly he insisted that faith should be personal, that it should involve one's whole life, not be a cobwebby crutch for times of trouble.

There is little doubt that much of Dietrich's new faith came from his ecumenical ties. The Student Christian Movement, led by John Mott, had at first bothered him; it had too much faith and too little theology. But in himself he saw too much theology and too little faith. In study papers, in addresses, and in devotional material, Dietrich increasingly accepted the authority of God not only over the world, but also over Dietrich Bonhoeffer.

In the summer of 1932, Dietrich prepared for the classroom some material on a subject that has become classic for almost every theologian: the opening chapters of Genesis. Some of his critics think it was in these lectures that Dietrich really discovered his faith. Previously he had talked of creation as a legend, and some of the students who had been with him for several terms immediately noted the change in his attitude and language. There was such loud shuffling of the feet, such general acceptance, that he extended his lectures.

For one whose specialty was New Testament systematics, lecturing on Old Testament isagogics should have made Dietrich uncomfortable, especially in the case-hardened atmosphere of the University of Berlin. At first he intended the lectures only for the classroom, for discussion, but the students urged him to consider publication. Eventually his work came out in print as *Creation and Fall.*

Like much of Dietrich's thinking, the book was timely in a country where the politics of Hitler and the Nazis were beginning to take over. He explained how the church should focus its activities if it wanted to rise above political partisanship. At first the readers for the Christian Kaiser Verlag recommended the manuscript not be accepted; they thought it too controversial. Then the publisher himself stepped in and printed it.

In addition to his loose ties to the University of Berlin, Dietrich was appointed chaplain to the Technical University at Charlottenburg. With the help of his sister Susanne and her friends, he organized a student center that was at the same time religious, intellectual, and social. It grew so quickly, he soon had to find bigger quarters. The costs for rent, food, janitors, heat, and light came from donations. For six months the center was hectic with parties, anniversaries, breakfasts, and dinners. There were also problems: lack of leadership, too much drinking, infiltration by the communists, and antagonism toward Jewish members. Then the Nazi election of early 1933 resulted in an order to close student clubs of every type.

Dietrich's life during these months was not wholly happy. Apparently he found himself too much of a theological orphan. The historical-critical scholars at Berlin considered him a Barthian, "a viper in the bosom," but the Barthians thought him a *historiker*—a historian. To celebrate Barth's 50th birthday, his former students prepared that most German of intellectual tributes, a *festschrift,* a collection of learned essays. Dietrich was not invited to contribute, a considerable blow to his pride, though he had never been one of Barth's students.

Twice Dietrich sought the pulpit of influential churches, according to the Reformed custom, with a trial sermon. At St. Bartholomew's he preached movingly and touchingly of Christ stilling the sea. He argued that present-day disciples were as fearful as Christ's had been, but for political reasons. An older pastor from Brandenburg chose the identical text, preaching no politics and including a host of anecdotes. The church session chose the older man, not Bonhoeffer. Such rebuffs depressed Dietrich, not only concerning his own abilities, but even more about the kind of world in which he lived.

Bonhoeffer's most controversial sermon—and he almost seemed to delight in being controversial—was one delivered on Reformation Day in 1932 at the Kaiser Wilhelm Memorial Church on the Kuhdam, where the rich and influential worshiped. Chancellor von Hindenburg was a member. In that sermon, Dietrich irritated conservative laypeople and Nazis alike when he said that Luther should be allowed to rest in peace: "The fanfares for the Reformation celebrations are the fanfares for a funeral. The day of Reformation celebrations has turned into an evil day." He went on to say that when people sang "A Mighty Fortress," they were merely calling on God to support their own evil causes.

He compared the Evangelical Church to Solomon's temple, once glorious but now in a state of ruin. Worst of all, it was the German Christians themselves who were tearing it down, stone by stone. The fault could not be laid at the feet of 100 pagan Babylonians. Naturally, this kind of preaching won Dietrich little support, however insightful it may have been. Some of his friends agreed with his point of view, but few thought the pulpit the proper place to proclaim it. This approach, they argued, was more suitable to the floor of the Reichstag or the columns of the newspapers.

One has to admire Dietrich for recognizing so soon the problems that Germany was facing, whether religious, cultural, or political. For one so young, his insight was unusually acute. What he lacked, however, was maturity and diplomacy, qualities he would need even more under the Nazis.

13

The Nazi Menace

The Great Depression deflated not only the world's stock markets, but also its politicians. It brought about the downfall of Herbert Hoover in America and of Paul von Hindenburg in Germany. Voters who were out of food, out of work, and out of patience wanted quick change. Seeking a paradise on earth, they elected Franklin Roosevelt in America and Adolf Hitler in Germany.

Serious illnesses sometimes require serious remedies. In America that meant shutting down banks, moving away from the gold standard, the birth of a whole alphabet of federal agencies, and price controls. Some of these actions the Supreme Court later declared unconstitutional. In Germany it meant no more free speech, no regular elections, no public assemblies, and loss of all rights for the Jews.

The German people had never really given the Weimar Republic a proper chance. They had lived too long under kings and emperors, and their brief experience with democracy was burdened by hard times and war debts. In 1933, the National Socialist Party won only a small plurality, but it promptly named Hitler head of government in the same month Franklin Delano Roosevelt took office in Washington.

If Dietrich Bonhoeffer had been concerned about militarism at Tübingen, he now had real reason to worry. The will of the people had been a long time gelling. Now they had a determined leader—a bachelor who claimed not to smoke, drink, or chase women, who smiled easily, who kissed babies, who supported the churches, who loved all things German.

The day after the election, Dietrich gave a short speech over the radio, as his father often did. He pointed out that young people often rallied round a charismatic leader, often an unworthy one. The speech did not even mention Hitler, but before his final sentences were broadcast, the station cut Dietrich off the air. Had he been censored, or had he simply gone beyond the time limit?

At first, National Socialism was greeted with enormous enthusiasm. Germany was searching for someone to save it. Cathedrals sprouted forests of swastika banners, and the pews were filled with brown-shirted worshipers. Yet there was no joy at Wangenheimstrasse. Rüdiger Schleicher muttered, "This means war."

Almost at once there was tension and distrust. New regulations poured from the government every week. That was the spring Paul Lehmann and his wife were visitors in Berlin. The Bonhoeffers kept tiptoeing to the hallroom doors, making sure the servants were not eavesdropping. There were almost daily telephone calls to Sabine at Göttingen because her husband was Jewish.

Four weeks after Hitler came to power, the Reichstag burned to the ground. The loss of the parliament building was symbolic. Exactly what caused the fire will probably remain one of history's mysteries. The man charged with the crime was a Dutch communist by the name of Van der Lubbe. He was only 24 years old. There was considerable suspicion that the fire had been started by the Nazis themselves, who then set up cordons to make sure no one could get in to put it out.

The loss of the Reichstag helped Hitler immensely. The propaganda line was this: If the Communist Party is strong enough and dedicated enough to burn down the parliament, obviously the country needs strong controls. The next morning Hitler issued the first of a long series of *Notverordnungen*, or emergency regulations. These put a serious crimp in the usual civil liberties: freedom of speech, freedom of the press, freedom of assembly, and freedom from unwarranted search.

Now the Nazis consolidated their power. At first the churches and the universities were not affected. The restrictive laws were applied only to the communists and social democrats. But Dietrich was considerably annoyed. His letters, telegrams, and phone calls were censored, a real imposition for one with so many contacts abroad.

Early in March 1933, Germany elected a new Reichstag. For the first time, the Nazis won the clear support of the people with 44 percent of the vote. With so many parties contending, the plurality was clearly a landslide and paved the way for 12 years of Nazi rule. To be genuinely popular, however, Hitler had to convince all the voters, not just 44 percent of them. Between acts of an opera at Bayreuth, he made extravagant appeals to the religious sensibilities of the German people, complimenting them, cajoling them, bullying them. He often appeared in public with leading churchmen, bolstering his claim to the hearts of loyal churchgoers, whether Protestant or Catholic.

Meanwhile new laws were continually surfacing. The Aryan clause excluded Jews from the civil service. Another decree prohibited Jews from managing a business. The worst was the Treachery Law. This outlawed any criticism of the state. Under such a law, one could not even discuss politics. Talking with foreigners was especially condemned.

Dietrich was in the middle of his creation and fall lectures, which he now filled with contemporary quotations and examples. He stated that evil was being born in the world at this very minute, sometimes with the help of well-intentioned people. He stressed the image of the serpent: how the Garden of Eden had been ideal until Satan invaded it. Although he did not name Hitler or the Nazis, he left little doubt about the implications.

Not long after the Nazi takeover, Dietrich preached a sermon on Gideon. With only a few men, Gideon had won the battle against the Midianites. The Israelites wanted to make him king. But Gideon fought off any claim to fame, saying, "God shall rule over you, and you shall have no other lord." Bonhoeffer concluded with a dramatic monologue of Gideon rampaging through the pagan shrines. Finally, he depicted Gideon kneeling and praying, "Lord, be thou our only God."

Dietrich still fostered close contact with his ecumenical friends. Almost as if it had been prophetic, the World Alliance of Churches and its Life and Work Committee had scheduled a conference in Berlin on the day of Hitler's election. Now the leaders of foreign churches could see for themselves what was happening in Germany. Churchmen such as Ammundsen and Henriod and Bell were swamped in a sea of swastikas decorating the Wilhelmsplatz. Some leaders of the German church, such as Dibelius and Deissmann, were more than happy to welcome the visitors, in part because they actually wanted them to see the spirit of the German people. Unabashedly welcoming the change in government, they did not foresee the excesses that were to come.

Almost from the start Hitler tried to win the Evangelical Church to his own camp. His approach to the Catholics was somewhat different. Catholic power originated in Rome. If he could make peace with the Vatican, he could eventually make peace with German Catholics. Later that summer, he signed a concordat with Rome. That did not mean he always lived up to it. As resistance mounted, equally as many Catholic priests as Protestant ministers swung from the gallows.

Not all churchmen valued freedom as highly as did Dietrich. When the pressures were concentrated primarily on communists and Jews, many clergymen remained silent. No one wanted the years of bloodshed that had gone on in Russia after the communists had seized power. Even Bonhoeffer did not worry excessively. Like the rest of his family, he did not expect Hitler's regime to last the year.

Unfortunately Hitler's political know-how was considerable. He took determined steps to worm his way into all the power structures, including those of the church. Early in April, only two months after the election, he assembled the electors of the Evangelical Church for a rare national conference. He promised his protection and said he wished to make the church the cornerstone of a strong German society. He also tried to win understanding for depriving the Jews and the communists of their civil rights.

Hermann Göring, Hitler's second in command and soon to be Reichs Marshal, also spoke to the assembly and argued for a well-organized church to support a well-organized Germany. This would require new offices and titles but not basic change. He also explained his political concept of a *Führer*, a man of strong conviction and moral principle who would have a free hand in restoring Germany to her proper place among the nations of the world. For the church, Göring proposed the office of a *Reichsbischof*. This *Reichsbischof* would assume a kind of central authority over the 28 regional churches. The Nazis already had a man in mind, Ludwig

Müller, a military chaplain stationed at Königsberg. Among churchmen he was almost totally unknown, and his crude grammar and harsh East Prussian accent made him sound like a country bumpkin.

The national conference supported only a few of the Nazi proposals. The delegates did agree the church needed a stronger authority, but not the kind proposed. For too many years, the 28 churches had all gone their own way, without enough cooperation and goodwill. Dietrich was bothered by all the politicking he saw among the churchmen even more than by the proposals themselves, without, intellectually, really knowing why. Karl Barth wondered aloud if he would ever be able to feel at home in this strange world of church politicking.

A three-man commission of bishops met in May at Loccum, an old monastery near Hanover, to discuss the reorganization. Hitler insisted on a special representative for the German Christian Party and appointed none other than Ludwig Müller. Now the four delegates focused not so much on reorganization as on the concept of a Reich church and why that church should support the Aryan clause.

Meanwhile, the universities were also experiencing the political pressures of the Third Reich. By May, faculties throughout Germany were being forced to join the party. Dr. Karl Bonhoeffer was proud that the psychiatric hospital was the only one at the university where there was no portrait of Adolf Hitler. Faculties that did not give in were labeled Jewish or Communist, or at least anti-German. On May 10, students across Germany demonstrated against Jewish intellectuals with massive book burnings, throwing into the fires the works of Sigmund Freud, Thomas Mann, Albert Einstein, and Erich Maria Remarque.

In the church, the Nazi activists were called "German Christians." The opposition, under a dozen different banners and names, amalgamated to some degree as "The Young Reformers." By June there was a German Christian Student Fighting League at almost every German university, groups which supported the principle of a *Führer* and a *Reichskirche*.

The battle seems to have been drawn most sharply on the campuses. At the University of Berlin, one meeting involved hundreds of students and at another, thousands. The first, organized by the German Christians, failed when the audience simply walked out. The second attracted 2,000 students and featured speeches by six professors. Although no vote was taken, the forum was a lively one. Bonhoeffer, one of the speakers, pushed for a full-scale church council, not unlike the ancient ones at Nicaea, where a wide representation of churchmen could take time to thrash out all the theological implications. What Dietrich proposed actually did happen a year later in the significant meetings at Dahlem and Barmen, but by that time, the action was too late. Meanwhile, Hitler simply went ahead with the appointment of Ludwig Müller as *Reichsbischof.*

The church president of Old Prussia, a Nazi supporter, immediately ordered services of thanksgiving and praise both at the National Cathedral and at the Kaiser Wilhelm Memorial Church, celebrations complete with Nazi flags and rites. Those church superintendents who objected were immediately dismissed, but still they arranged opposing services of penitence and contrition. As Dietrich saw it, however, the services at Berlin's two biggest churches, along with the signing of the concordat in Rome, gave Hitler the power over the churches he had been seeking. To Dietrich, the new regime was becoming a fire-breathing dragon, and he seethed inwardly when he cast about for a way to fight it without getting burned by its fiery breath.

14

A Divided Church in Germany

One summer was more decisive than any other for the career of Dietrich Bonhoeffer—the embattled summer of 1933, the year Hitler came to power. In May and June, Dietrich's lectures on Genesis had gone so well they made up for his inability to get a church of his own or a post as professor. During the student disruptions in June, Dietrich had emerged as something of a hero. His spirits rode high.

He was certainly not alone in his opposition to the *Reichskirche*. Karl Barth now entered the fray, quietly, with a sober magazine article. Like a sharp sword, he cut to the heart of the matter. Christians, he wrote, too often put their trust in men, men such as those of the German Christian movement, who wish to win by politics what God alone can give and that by grace and faith.

Although Barth was not physically in Berlin, his voice carried considerable weight. Thousands of clergy who were still undecided began to consider their positions. Part of the difficulty was that no one knew exactly what platform the German Christians supported. Besides, like the Bonhoeffer family, most Berliners expected the new regime to last only a few months. Dr. Bonhoeffer did not disguise his conviction that Hitler was psychiatrically too unstable to maintain control even of his own cabinet.

In the midst of this turmoil, the 27-year-old Dietrich got two calls. One was from a German congregation in London that needed a pastor. Would he come and preach a trial sermon? The other was from a committee of church superintendents. Would he go to Bethel and, with Hermann Sasse, help write a document for bargaining with the German Christians?

Both were valid requests, and both were exactly what Dietrich enjoyed. He accepted both. But first there was a church election. With two other young pastors, Dietrich activated the Young Reformers. From an office in Dahlem, they poured out pamphlets and posters trying to ensure the defeat of Ludwig Müller.

Dietrich borrowed his father's Mercedes and chauffeur and with a band of students plastered Berlin with posters. At first there was interference from the Gestapo, but Dietrich and another pastor boldly invaded its headquarters on the Prinz Albrecht Strasse, insisting on seeing the chief. Both parties had a legitimate complaint. The German Christians had secured a court order preventing the Young Reformers from using the name "The Evangelical Church." On the other hand, the Young Reformers had every legal right to campaign in a free election. So the phrase "Evangelical Church" was blotted off the posters and the Young Reformers were back in business.

The story of Dietrich's involvement in that early confrontation with the Gestapo was grossly exaggerated. From Sutz in Switzerland came a worried query whether Dietrich was being sent to a concentration camp. At this stage of the game, it was Bonhoeffer who was hounding the Gestapo, not the other way around. Dietrich insisted on his free rights in a free election, and he received them.

Even before the election, the regional superintendents realized that fighting the German Christians was a lost cause. Their judgment was right. The *Reichskirche* and the *Reichsbischof* won far more votes, on a percentage basis, than had Hitler himself. Bonhoeffer now got together with Franz Hildebrandt and suggested one of the quirkiest proposals of all: a strike. Why not? Pastors should simply refuse to bury the dead until the pressure from the people forced the *Reichsbischof* to resign. Older and more experienced heads argued otherwise. Was this the kind of stuff Dietrich had learned in America? At a Spanish bullring? Should pious mourners be cut off from God's Word simply because one did not like the bishop?

While the church was trying to decide what to do, Dietrich was thinking about what he and Herman Sasse should write at Bethel. By letter, by telephone, and by interview, he was seeking ideas that might challenge the new *Reichsbischof* and the German Christians. Meanwhile, there was also that trial sermon in London. He did not know if he wanted to leave Berlin at all, but the propaganda machine of the German Christians disgusted him. In fact, they had borrowed people and ideas from Hitler's political staff, snowing the church under a blizzard of newspapers, radio talks, and handouts. The students had been the only effective opposition, and as a student pastor, Dietrich recognized just how futile the whole situation was.

At the end of July, Dietrich caught the train to London and preached to the dual parish of St. Paul's and Sydenham. The first was a church of Reformed background, like the one at Barcelona. The other was a Union church, half Lutheran and half Reformed. In London, Dietrich also checked out the parsonage, a huge Victorian mansion that housed not only the pastor, but also a German school.

No matter how much the Londoners urged him to accept, Bonhoeffer was unsure of his feelings. The Anglican bishop of Ripon, a friend from Geneva meetings, reminded him that two or three scores of people sitting in the pews, mainly businessmen and diplomats, were not nearly so exciting as the academic and theological world of Berlin. Yet Dietrich would, over time, get to know the Church of England well and could help British churchmen interpret what was happening in Germany.

Without finally making up his mind, Dietrich headed back to Germany for the bargaining sessions at Bethel. He had never visited the community of Bethel, which took its name, "House of God," from the Old Testament. Friedrich von Bodelschwingh had founded it a generation earlier to care for epileptics. Now it had grown into one of the biggest medical complexes in Germany and included its own seminary and mission school. Visibly impressed, Dietrich recalled how Buddha had been brought to enlightenment by a dying man. Could Germany be enlightened by a new statement from this "House of God"?

A statement summarizing the church's stand could serve several purposes. It could be a tangible rallying point. It could smoke out the German Christians. It also could provide the superintendents time to organize resistance to the *Reichskirche*. To write a creed at Bethel was as difficult as it must have been for the early Christian church fathers at Nicaea. For one thing, the purpose was negative: to deny those emphases of the German Christians that were not scripturally sound. The framers, primarily Bonhoeffer and Sasse, with a dozen helpers, stressed the usual doctrines of the church—the Trinity, the work of Christ, the creation—and what was not so usual, the civil rights of all humankind, including the Jews. But the Confession of Bethel grew tedious and wordy. Dietrich complained that it was too "Lutheran." Its simplicity had vanished. The whole idea of encouraging two young theologians to write anything that would please their elders posed a real problem.

The conferees completed the initial draft on August 25. The original notion had been to mail copies to 20 of Germany's leading churchmen. They would edit it, and once the document was reasonably acceptable, sign it. Then the confession would be circulated throughout the church. Even a casual glimpse at the names of those 20 should have alerted the authors to roadblocks along the document's path to acceptance. Those 20 represented too broad a spectrum—in politics, in theology, and in churchmanship.

Dietrich was not satisfied with the Confession of Bethel even in its original draft. Now that it was drastically altered by the respondents, he was even more unhappy. The 20 church officials responded that it should not be issued at all, and if it were, should support the German Christians. Two more complained that it sounded too much like Karl Barth, though he had been nowhere near Bethel. Three proposed that Lutherans and Reformed sign separate documents. In any case, the final draft of the confession turned out to be so meaningless that even Sasse and Bonhoeffer, its authors, refused to sign it.

Sometime during the three weeks at Bethel, Dietrich made up his mind to accept the call to London, though there was at least one good reason to stay in Berlin. Professors who openly opposed the Third Reich were falling from their chairs like ripe plums. Dean Seeberg, Bonhoeffer's old mentor, now retired, gladdened Dietrich's heart by telling him he had been strongly considered for a faculty opening at the university, but of course he had decided to go to London now, had he not?

The riots in June, the electioneering in July, and the long hours of writing in August had exhausted Dietrich. He had not relaxed among the beeches of Friedrichsbrunn for nearly two years. He vacationed there after Bethel. Among the yellowing oaks and the graying lichen, he could again gather some of the wits that had seemed to fly off in all directions.

In September, the Evangelical Church in Germany finally knuckled under to the Nazis after six months of resistance. At Nürnberg there had been a huge rally, the Victory of the Faith, complete with bands and flags and songs and speeches. In a noisy aftermath at Berlin, the Prussian Synod met for what came to be called the Brown Synod. There, the brown shirts visibly took over, with half the clergy appearing in uniform, and swept out of office all the former superintendents.

The atmosphere was one of demonstration. Committees were not allowed to meet. Those who spoke against the German Christians were arbitrarily ruled out of order. On the Jewish question, there was still some indecision. The assembly voted to accept no more clergy of Jewish background, but it insisted on retaining those already ordained, men such as Franz Hildebrandt.

Such illegal tactics of the Brown Synod actually hurt the German Christians. The clergy felt trampled on. They realized they could no longer remain neutral, and a tidal wave of opposition rapidly swept through the church. Soon they put together the skeleton of the *Pfarrernotbund*, the Pastors' Emergency League.

The new organization resisted the *Reichskirche* in exactly the way Bonhoeffer had hoped when he was struggling with the Confession of Bethel. Perhaps the Emergency League won over thousands of the clergy because its platform was so simple: (1) to support the Scriptures and the historic creeds, (2) to resist doctrinal attacks, (3) to help any who suffered wrongful laws or violence, and (4) to oppose the anti-Jewish laws. The struggle was becoming so exciting that Dietrich hated to leave. Yet in one state after another, by fair means or foul, the superintendents were being replaced by German Christians. Only now, when it was too late, were some of the more gullible churchmen beginning to realize what was really happening.

Ludwig Müller, the new church head, was confident enough of his grasp on the religious tiller to start planning a glamorous and colorful coronation as *Reichsbischof*. His words were more prophetic than he knew: "The political battle for the church has ended. Now starts the battle for men's souls."

Meanwhile, Dietrich was tending to one last ecumenical chore before he left for England. As the youth delegate of the World Alliance, he attended a conference at Sofia in Bulgaria. There, he took an active part in formulating various resolutions, including one that condemned any political action that downgraded a people or race, as did Hitler's Aryan cause.

The German delegation was not altogether happy about Bonhoeffer's open flouting of the Third Reich. Even talking to foreign churchmen was technically a violation of the Treachery Law. The head of the German delegation was Dr. Theodor Heckel, a man not much older than Dietrich, who was external affairs officer. In other words, he controlled appointments such as those to the churches in London. Almost at once he pointed out that Dietrich now would not be permitted to go to London; how could anyone so outspoken represent his church abroad? Dietrich sought a quick appointment with the new *Reichsbischof*.

Practically, there was no point in harassing Bonhoeffer. He would be more troublesome in Berlin, stirring up all those young theologians, than in far-off Britain. Besides, his brothers, uncles, cousins, and father held top jobs in government and society. There also were the London churches to consider. Would they cause trouble if they did not get a preacher on whom they had set their hearts? Ludwig Müller was no *dummkopf*. There was far more reason to let Dietrich go than to try to stop him.

15

London

In mid-October, the ferry ride across the North Sea can be stormy and uncomfortable, with the wind whipping up the breakers and dashing spray over the scuppers. Dietrich Bonhoeffer was not so much thinking about the weather as about why he was going to England. He had never felt at home in America. The docks at Harwich or New York seemed far more alien than those at the Hook of Holland or Bremerhaven. Even back in Berlin he had felt strangely ineffective. Martin Niemöller, Gerhard Jacobi, and Herman Sasse, the very men he felt closest to, often thought him too youthful and immature. A few months earlier, he had had his heart set on that clergy strike, but even his admirers thought that notion a bit outlandish.

Was he right in running off to London? Where could he be most effective? Should he really be deserting the church struggle? Dietrich had written to Karl Barth, whom he considered a spiritual godfather, but boarded the train without waiting for an answer. When the answer came, Barth did not mince words. He was highly complimentary: Dietrich had been the most effective young man in the whole resistance and one who did not have to worry about pensions and retirement and supporting a wife. With a touch of rebuke, Barth suggested Dietrich was not yet old enough or bitter enough to withdraw under a juniper like Elijah or under a gourd like Jonah. He ought to be on the front lines. This was no time for retreat.

The overall tone of the letter struck Dietrich as somewhat harsh. Barth could fight from an ivory tower and, as a Swiss, could fall back to his homeland. Dietrich sent the letter to his father for a second opinion. In any case, he was now established in London, if only for a week or two, and was not ready to abandon his little parish. Dietrich's father made two points. One, London was close enough to Berlin to keep track of what was happening, and two, wars were not won by single skirmishes.

Perhaps for the first time in his life, Dietrich realized how much he differed from other 27-year-olds. He was shy and introverted. He did not trust his own judgment. Yet when he wanted, he could be charming and captivating. He had unusual gifts of intellect and language, but when riled, he could turn sarcastic and abrasive. He had no compassion for mediocrity or laziness. At home he always had so much attention that he came to expect it from everyone.

There was something obviously missing from his life. It was not a wife. He was not, on the whole, interested in women. It was not money. His parents were more than generous. What he seemed to be lacking was a goal, a purpose. He thought of himself as opportunistic—those journeys to Italy, Spain, the United States, and now England. There did not seem any good reason why he should have deserted his studies at Tübingen and switched to Berlin, except his own convenience. He did not appear to be getting anywhere, flitting from one place to another. His path was blocked to some of the things he really wanted: a teaching post in Berlin or a pastorate at a big church. After fighting Hitler for eight months, the one thing in life Dietrich had really enjoyed, he had now deserted the fray. He did not know whether to feel frustrated or guilty.

London must have been quite a change for Dietrich, despite its music and drama, its ballet and culture. He now had a parish of his own for the first time in his life. But compared even to the church in Barcelona, the two congregations were minuscule. The two tiny congregations counted scarcely more than 100 souls, and Dietrich seldom preached to a total of more than 50 people each Sunday. Both churches were declining in size as the bakers, butchers, tailors, and diplomats moved to the suburbs. While friends of Dietrich's such as Martin Niemöller and Franz Hildebrandt were preaching to thousands, he was preaching to dozens.

St. Paul's, nearly 200 years old, was situated just outside Petticoat Lane in Whitechapel. The parishioners there were mainly second- and third-generation immigrants, now more English than German. To a degree their church was a nationalistic club, and they were always hospitable toward refugees trickling in from Germany. The larger of the two churches was the one at Forest Hill, Sydenham, a half hour by train from the Liverpool Street Station.

The parsonage at Forest Hill was a Victorian monstrosity that would have made a good boardinghouse. The pastor lived in two huge rooms on the second floor. To make the place comfortable, his mother shipped over Dietrich's personal Bechstein, the grand piano that had nearly turned him into a concert pianist. Along with it came massive chairs and sofas, almost as if Dietrich had married and was setting up housekeeping.

So many of his friends and relatives piled into the parsonage during Dietrich's stay that it became something of a hotel. At Christmas, the guests included Dietrich's sisters Christel and Susanne and their husbands. One friend or another was almost continually dropping by. Dietrich also enjoyed using his rooms to practice a nativity play or a musical trio because they were warmer and more comfortable than the public rooms below. Here he also liked to play his African American spirituals for anyone who would listen.

Apparently Dietrich was both a night owl and a late-riser, when given free choice. The long discussions with Franz Hildebrandt, who arrived only a few weeks later to serve another London church and moved in with Dietrich, reinforced the pattern of going to bed late. Wolf-Dieter Zimmermann, a student of Dietrich's from Berlin, recorded in a diary that the usual schedule was to spend the evenings reading, writing, and discussing, usually until two or three in the morning. Unfortunately, Forest Hill was not on the subway. The buses and trains quit too early to take advantage of the West End plays and concerts. In the morning, by 10 or 10:30, someone brought in the *Times* and the milk. By 11 A.M. there was a festive breakfast: gammon, tea, kippers, eggs, baked tomatoes.

Life was not as comfortable as at Wangenheimstrasse. Dietrich and Franz fought a losing battle against the mice and had to store their food in tin boxes. The windows, huge and loose-fitting, faced the northeast, and when the wind blew off the North Sea, there was absolutely no way to keep warm. A gas grate in each room ran off a meter fed by shillings, but most Londoners could afford these only to take off the chill.

Even from 500 miles away, Dietrich was fascinated by what was happening in Berlin. Almost every night he was on the phone to Martin Niemöller or Gerhard Jacobi or to his politically oriented mother, who had sources of information in half the ministries. His salary was meager, and it was something of a family joke that it did not even cover the phone and telegraph bill, though the General Post Office gave him the cheaper commercial rates.

The Nazi government was consolidating its control far more quickly than even the most astute onlookers might have predicted. One clue was Hitler's prompt withdrawal from the League of Nations, an organization he thought had too strongly supported the hated Treaty of Versailles. In England, Dietrich played a worthwhile role as a spokesman for the resistance movement. From his ecumenical experiences, he already had solid entree into the Church of England.

He quickly became the spark plug of the five German pastors in London. They met regularly, at least in the winter, and were sometimes joined by the five who were stationed outside London. The parishes all belonged to the Association of German Evangelical Congregations in Great Britain and Ireland, headed nominally by a prominent banker, Baron Bruno Schröder. Under this banner, they cooperated in relief and welfare activities.

Since summer, the British newspapers had justifiably been giving Hitler bad press as the Nazis continued to whittle away at personal freedoms. By autumn, Hitler's control was even more assured, and his propaganda men were dreaming up ways to improve his image. Joachim Hossenfelder, the Prussian leader of the German Christians and a friend of the new *Reichsbischof*, wrote to St. George's, the largest German parish in London, and suggested he come to give a series of speeches. St. George's responded that the fall schedule was overcrowded. Instead, the visitor wrangled an invitation from Frank Buchman's Oxford Group for Moral Rearmament and from the Bishop of Gloucester. With Dietrich now on the scene to supply background and insight, the German pastors and most of the English ones boycotted Hossenfelder. His tour fell flat.

To win over the German pastors in London, the church affairs office in Berlin invited them to send a delegate to the installation of *Reichsbischof* Müller in December. On the surface, the offer was tempting—a free trip home for an underpaid and overworked clergyman. But the men in London, bolstered by Bonhoeffer, were adamant. They wanted no *Reichsbischof* and especially no Müller.

Practical as they were, the Germans in England discussed the invitation at their annual meeting. They even voted to send a delegate not to attend the inauguration, but to deliver in person their written objections. If the German Christians did not mend their ways, the English congregations would sever their ties completely. What really riled them were two incidents in Germany that happened that fall. One was the garish demonstration of Christian unity at the Sports Palace in Berlin on November 13. There the German Christians had organized a typical mass meeting in which 20,000 school children marched. Although advertised as a church rally, the affair had little to do with the church. All the party officials attended, including those of the Church Ministry. The stage looked more political than religious, with a Nazi banner as big as a basketball court as a backdrop. With brass bands, marchers, community singing, placards, and a goose-stepping battalion of Hitler's crack *Sturmabteilung*, or SA, the show got off to a rousing and flashy start.

The speaker was a prominent Nazi, the headmaster of a gymnasium. His speech shocked not only the youngsters, but their parents and pastors as well. He said that the Old Testament was a much overrated book about Jewish cattle traders and horse rustlers and ought to be thrown in the garbage can. Even the New Testament failed when it glorified guilt-ridden people like the Rabbi Paul. All the church really needed was a return to the historical Jesus, a man who had much in common with the ideals of the New Germany. When the spectacle finally ended, even the German Christians knew they had gone too far. Newspapers, pulpits, and classrooms echoed with complaints. The *Reichsbischof* objected that he was being stung to death by a swarm of hornets. He symbolically dismissed Hossenfelder, the head of the "Faith Movement of German Churches."

The other incident was not quite so brazen, but it was even more influential than the blasphemy at the Sports Palace. A decree was issued to merge all youth groups into the Hitler Youth. Obviously this was an appeal for the loyalties of the young. The order applied even to church organizations and those outside Germany. Dietrich was more than a little bothered by these strange goings-on, but he hoped in time they would wither away.

16

Deteriorating Relations

If Germany was the real stage for the theological fireworks, England at least put on a good sideshow. After Hitler installed Müller as *Reichsbischof* in January 1934, the church minister for external affairs promptly announced a trip to London. Theodor Heckel was carrying out orders. In proper fashion, he announced the trip not only to English pastors, the largest group in any overseas area, but to Bishop George Bell of Chichester, foreign relations man for the Archbishop of Canterbury, and to Baron Schröder, head of the German church association.

Before Heckel arrived, seven of the German pastors held a planning session. They were more than a little perturbed by the reports from Germany. They were even more perturbed by the instructions from Heckel's office to merge church youth into the *Hitlerjugend* and demanding the resignation of clergymen with any Jewish ancestry. They did not like the idea of a national bishop, they did not accept his authority, and they did not like this man reprimanding leading clergymen.

Heckel knew his visit would not be easy. He brought with him a theologian and a lawyer. What bothered him most was the statement the London pastors had written against the concept of a *Reichsbischof*. Yet the confrontation remained gentlemanly. First, Heckel's three-man team met with Baron Schröder, a tactic the pastors thought unfair, though apparently it did not poison the sessions that followed. Heckel then cited the change in church administration and the need for supervision and centralization. He outlined Hitler's genuine interest in organizing the Evangelical Church. He regretted that the efforts of the kaisers during the 19th century had not resulted in greater unity, but only in more squabbling and nit-picking. Even Luther himself, if he were alive, would throw up his hands in horror at so great a diversity among Protestants. Heckel also dropped an occasional threat into his talk. Pastors who were not cooperating with Hitler lost their parishes and their pensions. They were allowed to go into exile. Some, even those with as high a position as Martin Niemöller, continued to violate the Treason Law.

To a man, the London pastors raised objections. Could anybody who had sponsored so godless a demonstration as that in the Sports Palace really be a responsible Christian? Why was the Aryan clause so important when only those outside the church wanted it? Why was the Old Testament being thrown out the window? Why were preachers being told what they could preach and what they could not?

The pastors showed Heckel the paper they had worked out before his arrival. Politely he refused to take a copy back to Berlin, maintaining that it was too argumentative. He proposed, instead, that they examine his document, which said that the German church should work out its own problems without calling in outsiders.

The Londoners argued this was not the issue. The real question was whether the new leaders of the German church really were its leaders, and if they were, whether they were acting in a responsible way. Heckel suggested somewhat sarcastically that these pastors would wind up being *Prague émigrés*, the term for the communists who had successfully fled Germany after Hitler's election. At this, Bonhoeffer and two others walked out, but even the four pastors who stayed commented that Heckel's words were far from reassuring. So in a small way, the fight that was going on in Germany was duplicated in England. Heckel never out-argued the pastors. Neither did he persuade Bishop Bell or Baron Schröder. But at least the whole episode was conducted in a more gentlemanly fashion than the discussions in Berlin.

If Dietrich's contacts with the German church were somewhat unsatisfying, those with the Church of England were a pure delight. For 18 months, he cultivated a deep friendship with Bishop George K. A. Bell of Chichester. The two already knew each other casually because Bell was a central committee member of the World Alliance of Churches. In the Church of England, Bell held the additional post of foreign relations officer. A few months earlier, Dietrich had supervised the translation into German of the bishop's *Brief Sketch of the Church of England.*

Secretary Henriod of the World Alliance had written Chichester about Dietrich's arrival, reminding Bell of the lively young German who had made such a hit with his presentations at Sofia. First, Bishop Bell invited the newcomer to his club on Pall Mall, the Athenaeum, for a look into the world of gentlemanly London that not even many Londoners knew. Their talk was so cordial that Chichester immediately shipped off letters about Bonhoeffer to other leaders of the English church. From that point, the friendship between Bell and Bonhoeffer never ceased. They discovered they had the same birthday. They lunched together not only at the Athenaeum, and once or twice at St. James, but also at the ancient palace at Chichester. The bishop first thought Dietrich might prove a bit radical. Instead, he found him amazingly mature and a valuable source of information about the church struggles in Germany.

As a member of the World Alliance and also of the Church of England, the bishop found himself in a rather delicate situation. No matter what his personal feelings for Dietrich, he had to maintain a show of neutrality and open-mindedness. A Swedish bishop who also was a member of the World Alliance had sought an interview with Hitler, thinking perhaps the *Führer* did not understand quite how the German Christians and the Nazi philosophy were destroying the German church. But Hitler really did understand. He was not trying to help the church. He was merely trying to use it as a stepping-stone to power, just as he was using the military, the labor unions, the business establishment, and the universities.

Bell's influence in the World Alliance was perhaps greater than anyone else's. It was he who had presided over the conference at Novi Sad in Bulgaria, and it was he who also would sit in the chair next summer at the ecumenical conference to be held in Fano, Denmark. Despite the warmth between Bonhoeffer and Bell, there were genuine problems. The bishop did not want to give the impression he knew only one side of the church struggle. Dietrich was constantly being accused of poisoning the bishop's ear, potentially a serious charge under the Treason Law.

Several times the British newspapers sought to interview Dietrich about developments in the German church. Although he was willing to add further insight or details, he wanted to do nothing that would alienate him as a churchman. During the 1930s, the *London Times* ran detailed articles about what was happening in Berlin, usually from correspondents in Germany. More than once Dietrich was accused of writing such articles under a pen name. In fact, he generally avoided the press.

Dietrich's ties with the Church of England made him a marked man. Heckel of the External Affairs Office had talked to the Archbishop of Canterbury only a few minutes, only socially, and only at the Athenaeum. But Dietrich was a regular consultant at Lambeth Palace, the pile of bricks and stone that for centuries had been the London home of the Archbishop of Canterbury.

In February, Dietrich made a trip to Hanover to meet with the Pastors' Emergency League. Several weeks later, the External Affairs Office summoned him to Berlin. Heckel wanted to make certain Bonhoeffer was fully aware of the dangers of a pastor living outside Germany. He urged Dietrich to give up all ecumenical contacts because these were really the job of Heckel's office. Dietrich agreed to nothing. He even wrote his Swiss friend Sutz that he would make life as difficult as possible for Heckel.

The Nazis continued to make headway. They deposed the powerful head of the Westphalian Church, President Karl Koch. They closed seminaries. In a meeting at Ulm and another at Barmen, groups of pastors who opposed the takeover voted to withdraw from the state church. They called their new organization the Confessing Church. Some who strongly supported its goals preferred to think of it as a confessing *movement* rather than a confessing *church*.

Bonhoeffer did not participate in these two conferences, partly because he already had been absent so much from England, partly because he was under pressure from Heckel. The main draft of the Barmen Declaration was the work of Karl Barth and was heard like a church bell ringing through every German-speaking congregation. What it really condemned was a state-operated church that disregarded the witness of the Scriptures and arbitrarily decided matters of doctrine and practice.

That spring of 1934, hopes were strong that the National Socialists might fall. Dietrich was receiving regular reports from inside the chancellery, mainly from his brother-in-law Hans von Dohnanyi. The minister of finance had argued with the party and threatened to resign. Left-wing plotters continued to surface. In Austria, Prime Minister Engelbert Dollfuss was assassinated. But Hitler was clever enough to turn every plot to his own advantage. The most significant plotter was probably Ernst Roehm, who headed a coalition of Socialists, Communists, and various other malcontents, all eager to take over the government. The Nazi storm troopers and secret police struck first, however, on July 1, the "Night of the Long Knives." Scores and scores of every variety of political opponents were executed in cold blood that night, including one high-ranking marshal of the General Staff. Nobody knows exactly how many died—at least 70 and perhaps as many as 200. With the Nazis firmly in control of radio and press, the massacre was turned into a propaganda triumph, with the good guys winning over the bad guys.

The concept of shooting down political opponents without so much as a trial was normally as foreign to Germany as to any Western country. Yet this "Night of the Long Knives" was the climax of a string of political murders, recalling the years when a man might be shot for a cartload of bread or potatoes, when the real law of the land lay not with the Allied Control Commissioners somewhere in Paris, but in the hands of outlaws who carried carbines.

17

The Fano Conference

Throughout the spring of 1934, one year after Hitler had come to power, Dietrich Bonhoeffer was absorbed in preparations for the ecumenical conference that summer at Fano in Denmark. Fortunately, his duties in London were light. Now 28 years old, he had strong friendships in the World Alliance of Churches. In fact, his German friends occasionally suspected he had abandoned his deeply roving theology in favor of the socialized do-goodism of the ecumenicists. For Fano, Dietrich was scheduled to deliver a sermon, present a study paper, and organize the youth sector. For him, the conference was a not-to-be-missed opportunity to alert world Protestantism to the evils of Hitler.

In the few months since the Confession of Barmen, half the congregations in Germany and an even greater percentage of the clergy had joined the Confessing Church, the movement opposed to the *Reichskirche* of Ludwig Müller. Unfortunately, the men of the Confessing Church had no standing whatsoever in the World Alliance of Churches. Only the state church could participate in ecumenical affairs.

Karl Koch and Martin Niemöller, the two spark plugs behind the Confessing Church, asked Dietrich to serve as their negotiator with the World Alliance because he was on such good terms with the executive secretary and with the central committee. With only a few months until Fano, however, not even the World Alliance knew how to proceed. Was the Confessing Church really a church? Had it ever applied for membership? Could the World Alliance accept a splinter group, even if it wanted to?

In April, May, and June, letters, telegrams, and phone calls scooted back and forth across Europe. Theodor Heckel insisted the Confessing Church was not a legitimate church body, only a little church inside a bigger one, an *ecclesiola in ecclesia.* Dietrich wrote and phoned everybody he knew: Bishop Bell, Bishop Ammundsen, Secretary Henriod.

The bylaws of the World Alliance stated that each country and each church should determine its own delegates. The situation in Germany had no precedent, and neither of the two cochairmen, Bell or Ammundsen, wanted to overlook the Confessing Church. Neither did they want to make enemies of the *Reichskirche.* The final decision was to invite Karl Koch, not as a member, but as a guest, along with Friedrich von Bodelschwingh. This was not enough for Dietrich. Despite his friendship with Bell, he half decided not to participate, even as a staff member. Only after considerable persuasion did he finally leave for Denmark.

The conference at Fano turned out to be something of a landmark event. Dietrich's study documents focused so much on war and peace and were so political that the preparatory commission in Geneva watered them down. Yet the non-German delegates had been so influenced by the events in Germany of the past year—the ban on public discussion, the ousting of hundreds of church officials, the birth of the *Reichskirche,* the disregard for Scriptures—that they took an extremely forceful stand against the Third Reich and its oppression of the church. Although the *Reichsbischof* himself and several of his lawyers flew in by chartered aircraft, the final resolutions condemned the actions of the *Reichskirche.*

The conference at Fano outlawed the use of force in the church under any circumstances. It supported freedom of expression in pulpit and newspaper. It stressed the centrality of the Gospel. It pushed for free youth programs. It laughed at artificial definitions of race and blood. It encouraged the right to assemble.

Dietrich's successes at Fano were greater than even he had hoped. The frustration was that they made so slight a dent in the Nazi juggernaut. Dietrich's papers and sermon had been a ringing call to freedom, and the conferees responded with their votes and hearts. Even the youth delegates came through with wise and useful discussions, with resolutions even more forceful than those of their elders.

Dietrich had done his homework so effectively that there was even time for tennis and swimming. The island of Fano was famous for its sandy beaches and North Sea breezes. This was the kind of living Dietrich loved best. Even amid all this activity, Dietrich never forgot his sense of humor. A pastor from Berlin still cherishes a note Bonhoeffer wrote him while at the conference. A Russian bishop, a great ox of a man who had indulged for too many years in borscht and potatoes, with a huge cross dangling on his chest, had the floor. Dietrich scribbled down a quote from the German poet Christian Morgenstern:

Ein dickes Kreuz auf dickem Bauch,
Wer spürte nicht der Gottheit Hauch?
(A chubby cross on a chubby belly,
Who wouldn't feel the breath of God?)

Dietrich took his time leaving the continent. He did considerable politicking in Berlin and Würzburg, then visited Jean Lasserre at Artois, a laboring man's parish in France. The second half of his 18 months in London must have been anticlimactic after the success at Fano. Now Dietrich had become fairly well known in ecumenical circles, even within the German church, where 28-year-old heroes were still a mark a dozen.

There were more visits in London from Theodor Heckel. There were more resolutions from England against the *Reichskirche*. By now, political refugees who had fled the Third Reich were flooding into England. As early as September, there was a request that Dietrich consider returning to Germany to found an informal seminary.

Dietrich's pipe dream that winter, in the fogs of London, was still a journey to India. He had never given up his visions of studying under Mahatma Gandhi, of living and worshiping at an ashram. He talked Julius Rieger, one of the other young pastors in London's East End, into accompanying him.

Dietrich wrote his friend Sutz and his brother Karl-Friedrich that the jaunt was scheduled for the first three months of 1935. Always fond of his grandmother, he confided in her even more than in his parents. He was quite sure that Western civilization was going down the drain, that the population explosions of India and China would eventually guarantee them world power, and that Christianity was in danger of dying.

His friends thought Dietrich a little mad. Hildebrandt and Jacobi argued about the time and energy such a trip would take out of him. Karl Barth wrote that a trip to India would be crazier than the one to London had been. Reinhold Niebuhr, his mentor at Union Seminary, drew up a proposed study program and obtained a personal invitation for him from Gandhi. But Niebuhr also commented that a sophisticated theologian from Berlin would in one week get tired of sitting around on the smelly earth of India and would ask himself why he had ever left the drinkable water and the edible food of the West, a strong argument for one so hygienic and health-oriented as Dietrich.

Bishop Bell wrote to Gandhi, stating that Dietrich was particularly interested in learning something about passive resistance and about community. Bell's letter described him as genuine and earnest, a true seeker. Gandhi immediately responded with a letter of welcome. Bonhoeffer and Rieger could live in the ashram and travel with Gandhi as he journeyed throughout India. What Dietrich was really looking for, of course, was something he could apply to the church struggle in Germany. The question of whether passive resistance could really stop crack *Sturmabteilung* troops and tiger tanks never entered his head. In any case, the trip to India never came off. The congregations in Britain were receiving increasing static from Heckel, and Dietrich did not want to desert them. Besides, except for Rieger, he could find almost no one who thought the expedition worthwhile.

Dietrich increasingly thought about the preachers' seminary the Church of Old Prussia wanted him to start in April 1935. Since his first trip to Rome, he had had a secret hankering to be a monk. Now he made the rounds of the Anglican monasteries, many of them little changed since the Reformation, aided by letters from Bishop Bell. Maybe some good ideas would rub off on him, even if they were not as good as those he might find in an ashram with Gandhi.

As he wandered about England, Dietrich absorbed ideas wherever he visited. He admired the prayer groups among the Methodist theologues and the long silences among the Quakers. He visited five Anglican training centers and was especially impressed by those of the Cowley Fathers and the Mirfield Fathers.

Almost from the start, he began to wonder whether Luther had been right in being so hard on monks.

Dietrich liked the camaraderie of Christian ordinands living together. He kept the daily offices. He chanted the psalms. He meditated with the community. He heard the Scriptures read aloud. All these practices he stored away in his head, wondering if they could be adapted to his preachers' seminary. Now he was ready to head back to Germany. For 18 months, Dietrich Bonhoeffer had lived in England, not counting the half dozen trips to the mainland. Would he even recognize the fatherland? Had it become such a center for intrigue and tyranny and the trampling of human rights that he would want no part of it?

18

The Preachers' Seminary

Spring comes late to the shores of the Baltic, with the wind whistling across the dunes and slapping against the beaches. When the gales relax and the sun breaks out, however, the sky is bluer and the air brighter than anywhere else in Germany.

At the end of April 1935, Dietrich Bonhoeffer arrived at Zingst, a resort village on a hook of land sticking out into the Baltic. The manor house was a beauty, a mile out of the village, huddling at the edge of the forest with a cluster of cabins, a minute's walk from the sea. Awaiting him were 23 seminarians in their early 20s, Dietrich's assistant, Wilhelm Rott, and Wilhelm Niesel, an official of the Confessing Church.

The manor belonged to a Bible society in the Rhineland. By mid-June, when the sun was warmer and the trees in full leaf, the preachers' seminary would have to move to its permanent quarters at Finkenwalde, 90 miles to the east, to make way for the summer tourists. A work party already had left for Finkenwalde to clean and paint the place. But Zingst was a good place to start. The setting was ideal, the quarters comfortable, and the view to the islands inspiring.

The whole idea of a preachers' seminary was somewhat radical, born out of the church struggle. By order of the Third Reich, the regular seminaries of the church of the Old Prussian Union had now been closed for a year. With the Nazi disruptions at the universities, the flow of future preachers came to a halt. To guarantee a supply of clergy, the Confessing Church set up five "preachers' seminaries."

One of these was Bonhoeffer's, which would operate for six weeks at Zingst, then move to Finkenwalde. Dozens of sites had been examined, including several by Dietrich himself on jaunts back from London. They ranged from Lake Constance on the Swiss border all the way to the Baltic Sea. Finkenwalde was a village across the harbor from Stettin, sheltered from the worst of the storms, with a protected shoreline. The beech woods along the River Oder gave it its name: "the forest of the finches."

The manor house had once been magnificent, but its character had been spoiled by a nearby gravel pit. During its years as a private school, the estate also suffered the addition of a rather ramshackle gym. With the Nazi rules against private schools, the manor now stood empty. Although in need of endless buckets of paint, the place had distinct possibilities. Some of the old furniture was still in place, including two grand pianos. What other furnishings were needed were quickly supplied by the pious Junkers of Pomerania.

The Nazis proved a hidden blessing to Finkenwalde. Churchgoers all over the countryside were quick to pitch in with labor, food, and cash. With scrub brushes, whitewash, and cloth of Hessian blue, the gym made a respectable chapel. Up front in gilded wooden letters was the Greek word *hapax*, symbolizing the Christ who died once for all.

Inside the house, the ladies of the neighborhood brightened things with slipcovers and curtains. On the walls went Bonhoeffer's reprints of Rembrandt's biblical paintings, along with a favorite icon from Bulgaria. From Berlin, Dietrich brought his library, a fine collection of dogma and commentaries, including the vast Erlangen edition of Luther he had inherited from his Grandfather von Hase. He also brought his collection of records, not only the classics of Haydn, Mozart, and Beethoven, but also the more exotic church music of Schutz, Sweelinck, and Bach. And, of course, there was that unusual assortment of African American spirituals from the United States.

What characterized the preachers' seminary more than its furnishings was the concept of communal life, with students and faculty under the same roof. At a university, the students normally lived in rented rooms, at home, or at a fraternity. Here there was no choice. One lived with his fellows, studied with them, worshiped with them, swam with them, and ate with them. On the surface the togetherness was highly inviting. For Bonhoeffer, it provided a magical opportunity to put into practice some of his monastic ideals: common reading, worship, prayer, meditation, contemplation. He later described this in two of his books, *The Cost of Discipleship* and *Life Together*. For the students who could adapt, the seminary was a highly rewarding chance to grow. Unfortunately, there were some who balked.

Imitating what he had seen at English monasteries, Dietrich set up the main offices, or periods of meditation, for breakfast, dinner, and supper. Except for Sundays and holy days, worship usually took place in the dining room around the tables. The morning office was the most significant. Breakfast was always rather sparse at Finkenwalde, despite the filling food available from the Pomeranian countryside: bread, butter, marmalade, cafe au lait, maybe some porridge, but no eggs, no bacon, no sausage. At breakfast came the day's main devotions: readings from the Old and New Testaments, two chorales, an antiphonal psalm, a Gregorian chant, and an extemporaneous prayer, which was almost unknown in the German churches.

What the students rebelled at most was the half hour of silent meditation. There was no talking, no reading, no smoking (despite Dietrich's fondness for tobacco), no fidgeting, and no shoe shining—only sitting and thinking. On more than one occasion, the silent meditation caused a rebellion, and it was seldom observed when Dietrich was absent on one of his frequent trips. To him it was as essential as anything the students were learning in the classroom. He was constantly repeating the creed of a house of brothers: how they should support and encourage one another and how they should continue to meditate together. On that subject there was no casting of votes.

Dietrich was less successful in persuading the students to eat their heavy meal in the evening. His conviction was that too much food made one sleepy and eating heartily at noon brought the day too quickly to an end. As at monasteries, there was also a public reader, declaiming aloud from some worthwhile book of the times. The students rather enjoyed the readings but insisted Dietrich should not try to resist the centuries-old tradition of dinner at noon.

One Sunday each month, Dietrich conducted a Communion service. On Saturday night, Catholics had at one time come to their priest for private confession. The trace of this custom in Lutheran practice had been to talk privately with the pastor on Saturday night. Dietrich did not require the students to confess to one another, but he strongly encouraged it. For his own confessor, he chose a student from Saxony who was later to become friend, nephew by marriage, biographer, and literary executor, Eberhard Bethge.

The ideas Bonhoeffer brought to his preachers' seminary were not entirely welcome to men so young. As one student described it, they resisted like asses. They were not used to worshiping three times a day, singing Gregorian chants, reading at meals, and hearing one another's confessions. In housekeeping, almost no one could come up to Dietrich's standards. Under Spartan conditions, they did their own dishwashing and bed-making, with more than a few shirkers.

Already at Zingst, Bonhoeffer had made the point that each of them should do his share of dishwashing. When most of them settled, instead, around the piano or at the Ping-Pong table, he locked himself in the kitchen and admitted no one until the whole stack of dishes for 26 people was gleaming clean. At Finkenwalde, more than one student was embarrassed to discover that his unmade bed had been made by Dietrich himself, with the sheets as tight and the corners as square as if it had been made by an army cadet.

Every week Dietrich rode the train or drove his car or motorcycle to Berlin to teach his classes at the university. When he returned to Finkenwalde, he was something of a talking newspaper. Often he sat on the steps of the manor while the students gathered round to hear the news. At the end of the term, he brought back word that the Confessing Church would shortly be declared illegal. There was dead silence, then a buzz of questions. Would the students be thrown out? Would the seminary be closed? Where would they go?

That same autumn, Dietrich broke off the only real romantic interest there had been in his life. It was with a cousin, or perhaps a second cousin, the one he had often taken to plays and operas. No one ever wanted to identify her, and her name appears in none of his biographies. In any case, Dietrich was seldom in Berlin and had been gone in London for 18 months. Under other circumstances, he might have made time for romance, but now he finally had found a job that challenged him: running a seminary and establishing a community.

Meanwhile, the Old Prussian Union was hearing odd reports of what was happening at their preachers' seminary: Gregorian chants, private confessions, icons, African American spirituals, and worship three times a day, and not in a chapel, but at the table. Much of what they heard came from Dietrich himself. He proposed forming an informal House of Brothers, partly modeled on the *Brüderrat* of the older pastors.

The grayer heads were somewhat skeptical. To them, this was a kind of *Schwärmerei*, the term Luther had once used for radical faith and doctrinal mishmash. Wilhelm Rott, Bonhoeffer's assistant, who was more Reformed than Lutheran, also had strong doubts about the program, though he was diplomatic enough to keep his peace. In any case, the informal band of brothers was somewhat organized, and later assisted the families of those who were imprisoned in concentration camps.

The outlawing of the Confessing Church again brought the Finkenwalders into action. Martin Niemöller had published a massive protest against the state church, at considerable expense, and shipped copies throughout Germany. The Gestapo ordered booksellers to destroy them. Fortunately, the police order traveled through the mail, while Dietrich got his information by telephone.

Immediately he split his students into teams and sent them foraging through every bookstore in Pomerania, buying a copy here, four there, eight somewhere else. Just for the fun of it, and to outfox any police who might have a sharp eye, they changed costumes, took glasses off, switched caps, and appeared one time on a bike, then on a motorcycle. In a short time, they had a whole tableful of copies at the seminary at Finkenwalde. Using addresses found in church directories, they anonymously mailed copies to every churchman in the country, smirking a bit at the way they had outwitted the Gestapo.

With more and more trouble brewing, even Finkenwalde did not go unscathed. The outlawing of the Confessing Church made each of the seminarians review his own loyalties. At least one of them deserted, a real blow to Dietrich. Besides, the first class had now graduated, and he had to break in a new one in the middle of winter. The graduates scattered to the parishes of Pomerania, Brandenburg, and Saxony and awaited a personal visit of encouragement from their rector.

As if this did not already crowd his hectic schedule, Dietrich's grandmother died. Julie Tafel Bonhoeffer was that grand old lady who had looked after Dietrich and Christine at the university in Tübingen, who had encouraged his plans to visit India, and who had marched through a *Sturmabteilung* cordon to shop where she wanted, even if the store were Jewish.

Dietrich delivered her funeral address on January 15, 1936. For his text he used Psalm 90, which speaks of the Lord as our dwelling place from one generation to another. It was the psalm the family always read together at their New Year's dinner. Yet even at the funeral, the 29-year-old preacher did not downplay his political convictions. He said that what was right and good could not be twisted or bent. He praised his grandmother's clarity of thought and gentle speech, her upright life and direct simplicity. He reminded his hearers that she had not deserted the Jews when the government declared them out of favor. He finished with a ringing conclusion that her kind of world would not disappear with her into the grave. At least one cousin who attended the funeral thought the sermon too political and refused to shake Dietrich's hand.

Funerals were still private enough that a well-thought-of clergyman did not get thrown in jail simply for standing in the pulpit and preaching at one. But what happened the following month the authorities could not so easily swallow. That was Dietrich's notorious expedition to Sweden. It started at a boisterous birthday celebration at the manor house. Dietrich had just turned 30, an age he considered terribly old. The party was informal, gathered around the massive brazier of chestnut and copper that Dietrich had shipped from Barcelona. The students talked about birthday presents, a custom they thought pleasant but rather self-serving. Why didn't the one whose birthday was being celebrated *give* presents rather than *get* them? What could Dietrich give them?

They always had liked his talk of travel: Barcelona, New York, Morocco, Italy, Cuba, Mexico. Now Bonhoeffer responded with a surprising suggestion. How about a trip to Scandinavia? Not only for sight-seeing, but so the students could tell their Lutheran brothers what was really happening in Germany.

There was a bank regulation against taking marks outside Germany. With all his ecumenical contacts, Dietrich could circumvent that. Yet he did have a problem keeping the students' enthusiasm under control. Could a professor who had never sworn the oath of loyalty, along with a band of students from an illegal seminary, actually get an exit permit to visit the archbishops of Denmark and Sweden?

Despite these hurdles, the always-traveling Dietrich wanted to go and saw no valid reason not to take his students with him. He cautioned them on the need for discretion, if they indeed received an exit permit. A welcoming letter from Denmark and Sweden came by return post, with the help of the Swedish ambassador, the same man who had cautioned Hitler against oppressing the church. A minor official signed the German exit permit as if it were the traditional request of schoolboys off on a holiday. A week later, the seminarians boarded a ship at Stettin and sailed to Copenhagen. They were received by the archbishop and welcomed in numerous homes and parishes. Bonhoeffer delivered a series of lectures, not only about what was happening in the German church, but also about his concepts of a seminary.

The Swedish half of the jaunt was not so ordinary as the Danish one. The group scarcely had landed when the local newspapers were filled with stories of illegal seminarians fleeing Germany, an interpretation that was not at all true. It stirred up a hornets' nest back home. The Foreign Office, the Ministry of Education, and not the least, the church's Foreign Affairs Office quickly began an investigation. The students did have a legal exit permit, they discovered, but nobody quite knew how it had been approved.

In Stockholm, the German ambassador welcomed them icily under a life-size portrait of *Der Führer*. Everybody else acclaimed them as heroes. The two royal princes of Sweden, Eugen and Bernadotte, gave a reception and showed them the palace. In the ancient cathedral town of Uppsala, the archbishop treated them as warmly as the biblical prodigal son. Everywhere there was friendly conversation with fellow theologians, with perhaps a little too much publicity.

The 10-day swing through Denmark and Sweden was a delight both for the students and for Dietrich. Unfortunately, it advertised him as a man who did not mind fighting the regime. This kind of publicized resistance was what the *Reichskirche* hated most. It was far more visible than the private comments of some quiet little preacher or professor.

Dietrich was scarcely back in Finkenwalde when the wheels of the *Reichskirche* began to grind against him. He lost his lectureship at the university. That would have happened anyway, given his political views and criticism of the Nazis, but the trip to Scandinavia hurried it. He had long refused to take the oath of loyalty to the Third Reich, for the sake of conscience, or even fill out the questionnaire. Now Bishop Heckel reminded the authorities that Dietrich was both a pacifist and an opponent of the party. He should certainly not be allowed to teach in Berlin and probably not even at a preachers' seminary.

19

1936

Buried in the beeches and firs of Pomerania, the seminary poured out a steady stream of preachers. There were two classes per year and 20 or more men per class. Dietrich had every reason to feel that he was being useful and productive, that he had found his niche in life. What really made him glow inwardly—and he was not easily moved by emotion—was the way he had won the loyal support of the Pomeranian landholders. These Junkers had first settled there after the Crusades. Through his grandmother, Dietrich himself carried Junker blood.

The guardian angel who breathed fire and warmth into the Finkenwalde seminary was an elderly widow by the name of Ruth von Kleist-Retzow. Both she and her granddaughter were to play an important role in Dietrich's life. A strong-willed matriarch, Ruth von Kleist-Retzow represented all that was best in the nobility: simplicity, piety, authority, culture, and goodwill. To her, the coming of the seminary was a godsend. Too long she had seen the church on its deathbed, and all these young theologues so close at hand inspired her.

The estate of the Kleist-Retzow family lay at Klein Krossin, but most of the time, the grand old lady ruled her roost from a palatial town house in Stettin. Every Sunday morning she loaded up several cars with grandchildren and drove across the Oder to worship and eat with the seminarians. She also influenced the neighboring gentry—the Kleists, the Schmenzins, the von

Schlabrendorffs—so Dietrich and the seminary were an honored addition to the community.

The landowners found in Bonhoeffer those qualities they tried to nurture in their own offspring: nobility, intellect, ambition, an aristocratic bearing. As a pious people, they considered their lands the Lord's, and because the seminary was the Lord's doing, the harvest belonged to Him as well. Cartloads of food appeared at the seminary: cabbages, beets, potatoes, carrots, apples, pears, chickens, pigs, and quarters of beef.

At the town house in Stettin, Frau von Kleist set up a boarding school for her grandchildren while their parents were managing the estates. Her rule was almost as monastic as the one at the seminary, with prayers, Bible readings, and sermonettes by the duchess herself and sometimes by Dietrich. At the table and in class, the only language was French, as it had been in the court of Frederick the Great two centuries earlier. A continual flow of guests visited the house—artistic, musical, religious, and literary.

Frau von Kleist sent two of her grandsons to the seminary so Dietrich could instruct them for confirmation. They were bright boys and he always enjoyed teenagers. All three liked the experience, and the grand old lady wished all her grandchildren could study under him. A little doubtful about age, she brought over a blue-eyed granddaughter, still only 12, Maria von Wedemeyer. The girl was attractive and strong-willed, Dietrich noted, just like her grandmother, but still too immature for confirmation classes.

Despite the pleasant life and the weekly jaunts to Berlin, Dietrich occasionally felt frustrated when he began visiting his graduates, who were scattered all over eastern Germany. In his Mercedes, he looked like a bishop, but on his motorcycle, he looked like a playboy. He took delight in simple things. One student outlined in his diary a typical visit: meeting with the elders, preaching in church, eating a simple meal in a country inn, and swimming in the lake.

Yet the loss of the Berlin lectureship and, what was worse, the almost complete takeover of the university by the Nazis genuinely disturbed Dietrich. To the student who was his confessor, Eberhard Bethge, he called it by its medieval name: *tristitia*—sadness, depression. The monster that was the *Reichskirche* appeared invincible. The power of God seemed to be chained up. Once Dietrich got into trouble even when the fault was not in the least his.

The Swedish venture had been his own doing, true enough, but this scrape was caused by a couple of immature students, Werner Koch and Ernst Tillich.

It all started in Berlin in March 1936. The leaders of the Confessing Church saw a ray of hope that Hitler might be more conciliatory than his advisers. They prepared a study paper. They asked some hard questions and wanted some hard answers. Bonhoeffer, off in Pomerania, was too far away to be involved. The questioners promised Hitler complete secrecy, but they did request a response. They listed their complaints, sealed the document, and hand-carried it to the chancellery.

Ten weeks went by, and there was no answer. The leaders soon realized they would never receive an answer. The Third Reich and its *Reichskirche* did not want to go on record. Then the paper and questions showed up in newspapers at Basel, Switzerland, and London. Immediately, the Confessing Church offered an apology. Obviously there had been a violation of confidence and of the Treason Law, which forbade the relaying of information about German affairs to foreign media, but it had not leaked the information and did not know who had.

The Gestapo went to work. It learned that two of Dietrich's students had taken the document from a Berlin safe, copied it, and made a dramatic play for ecumenical support. Both were sentenced to a year in the concentration camp at Sachsenhausen, becoming the heroes of the Finkenwalde community. Yet the incident brought a new cloud of suspicion over Dietrich, though he was wholly uninvolved.

An article Bonhoeffer wrote that summer also stirred up a controversy. He used the phrase *extra ecclesiam nulla salus*, "outside the church there is no salvation." His argument went this way: If the Confessing Church is the true church, and if the *Reichskirche* is not, then can anyone in the *Reichskirche* be saved? The question was obviously controversial. It splattered across the front pages of the daily newspapers. The thesis was indeed radical, as Dietrich meant it to be. In his judgment, the *Reichskirche* had gone too far, and for him, the time had come when churchmen should resist, not knuckle under.

In the summer of 1936, Hitler wanted to put Germany's best foot forward. That was the year Berlin hosted the summer Olympics, and visitors streamed in from all over the world. The

Nazis wanted to make a good impression, and in fact there was much of which to be proud: the great system of public schools, the mushrooming of autobahns, the modernization of the railways, and the countless new apartments and factories.

Nor was religion neglected. One of the star guests at the Berlin Olympics was Dr. Frank Buchman from England, leader of the Oxford Movement, who publicly praised Hitler for saving the world from the evils of communism. Near the stadium, the *Reichskirche* erected a massive tent, asking leading preachers from all over the world to fill the pulpit.

Even Dietrich was caught up by the enthusiasm of the Olympics. He agreed to preach in the *Paulikirche*. There he faced the largest congregational audience of his life, and in fact had to repeat the service to let all hear. Inwardly, however, he distrusted the whole aura of religiosity and national pride at the Olympics and wondered if he was doing the right thing by participating.

Despite the efforts of the Gestapo to keep things under control, there were strange signs plastered on the walls. One of these stated:

> *Nach der Olympiade*
> *Hauen wir die Bekennende Kirche zu Marmelade*
> *Dann schmeissen wir die Juden raus*
> *Dann ist die Bekennende Kirche aus.*
> (After the Olympics
> We'll chop up the Confessing Church into marmalade
> Throw out the Jews
> And that'll be the end of the Confessing Church.)

A little of the agitation was schoolboy fun, though not very funny. Some of it was deadly serious. The conflict had reached an explosive point, and the Third Reich blithely encouraged it. Dietrich saw the picture clearly. One of his students once asked if a person couldn't be an honest member of the *Reichskirche* and simply ignore the things that were wrong, rather than join the Confessing Church. Dietrich's answer was classic. "If you boarded the wrong train, could you get where you wanted by running through the corridor in the opposite direction?"

The preachers' seminary at Finkenwalde had one more year of life, though in the summer and fall of 1936 its students felt it would go on forever. After a year's experience, the school was running smoothly, the lectures were in good shape, the buildings painted, the supply of food steady. In these quiet months, Dietrich settled down to write what would prove to be his most popular book, *The Cost of Discipleship*. The German title was *Nachfolge*, which means "following, discipleship" (a *Nachfolger* is a successor, disciple, or place-taker). Based largely on a series of lectures, the book concentrated on the Sermon on the Mount.

What made the book popular was the questions it raised. What does God want of us? What does it mean to be a Christian? How can one best serve God? These were the queries Augustine and Boniface and Aquinas and Luther had asked in their day. Now the questions were being raised in the context of Nazi Germany. Another concept that made the book popular was that of "cheap grace." Grace, said Dietrich, is costly, not cheap. God's grace, though free and unmerited, was not poured out without a tremendous price that was paid. The redemption of humankind cost Christ His life. Confessing the faith may cost us our lives. Faith is not only a meager hope that one wants to be saved. It is a wholehearted confidence in Christ and dedication to His mercy and daily providence. That kind of grace, that kind of faith, certainly is not without cost or cheap. Dietrich would experience the truth of his rich insight into the Gospel personally.

20

Underground Dissention

In the golden glow of the 1936 Olympic Games, the Gestapo chose to handle the Confessing Church with kid gloves. One year later, in June 1937, storm troopers invaded a meeting of the *Reichsbrüderrat*, imprisoning six of Germany's most influential pastors. General Superintendent Martin Niemöller had asked other outstanding clergymen, including Bonhoeffer, to come to his house for a session of brainstorming. Niemöller and his assistant, Franz Hildebrandt, had not yet returned to the parsonage from church when there was a pounding on the parsonage door and a breathless warning that the police were on their way. Niemöller already had been captured at church. Soon the police had surrounded the parsonage and demanded entrance.

For seven hours, Frau Niemöller and a half dozen pastors sat incommunicado in the parlor while the police ransacked the house for evidence. All they could find was a wall safe behind an oil painting with 30,000 marks belonging to the Pastors' Emergency League. On the streets outside, a large Mercedes-Benz purred by regularly, with Frau Paula Bonhoeffer peering out behind the chauffeur to observe what was happening.

The parish served by Niemöller and Hildebrandt was stubbornly loyal. The women's choir gathered beneath the windows and sang chorales to those inside. Only at the end of the day did the police finally leave, releasing the pastors, though Niemöller was to remain a prisoner for seven years. Meanwhile, Hildebrandt stirred the wealthy St. Anna's (or *Annenkirche*) congregation at Berlin-Dahlem to massive protest. One Sunday the people found the doors of the church locked. A big crowd assembled on the square. The police ordered them to disband. Instead, they formed a protest march, peaceful but noisy. Two hundred and fifty were arrested that day, including Pastor Hildebrandt, who was soon released.

The Ministry of Religion also began to pressure Dietrich's graduates. By Christmas, 27 of them were in jail. Technically, they could serve no parishes other than those of the state church. Increasingly, the Confessing Church was falling to pieces. One young pastor after another wrote Dietrich his tale of woe: Should he knuckle under and join the *Reichskirche,* or should he not be a pastor at all? In September 1937, while Dietrich was away between terms, the police sealed the doors of the seminary and imprisoned the assistant rector, Wilhelm Rott. Dietrich was not surprised. The doors already had been bolted on three of the other five preachers' seminaries.

By now pastors everywhere were being pressured to sign a loyalty oath to the *Führer*. After two months in jail, Rott was released from prison. Dietrich celebrated with an opera party to see *Don Giovanni* in Rott's honor. That week Berlin was filled with red-and-black swastikas and the rumble of tanks. This was a welcome not for Rott, but for Mussolini, who had conquered Ethiopia.

What should Dietrich do now? The senior pastors of the Confessing Church were behind barbed wire. The seminary at Finkenwalde was closed and the students had nowhere to go. The decision had to be Dietrich's. He was nothing if not a schemer. He suggested to two church superintendents of Outer Pomerania a highly acceptable proposal, a *Sammelvikariat,* or group vicarage. Near Köslin and Schlawe, a hundred miles east, many churches could use an assistant. Why not split the student body into two groups? They could study together, help out on Sundays, and appear on the police books as assistant pastors.

The idea worked. Dietrich spent half his time at Köslin, half at Schlawe, 25 miles apart. In winter he drove his Mercedes, in summer his motorcycle. The worst problem was the snow, which sometimes for weeks cut off food, mail, and coal deliveries. Living in the forest was a delight for Dietrich. When a pastor at Schlawe married and needed the parsonage, the students moved to Sigurds-hof. There they occupied a hunting lodge on a ducal estate.

Life in the real world was more grim than in the fairylands of the Baltic. The struggle between those who thought pastors should compromise and those who thought they should fight, between the *Reichskirche* and the Confessing Church, simmered on. The glory days of Finkenwalde were past, even if Frau von Kleist did continue to play the grand hostess, even if the *Sammelvikariat* did carry on for another two years.

Churchmen everywhere were now restricted from traveling, and the police kept a sharp eye mainly on those who were influential. The purpose of the ban was to stop mass protests. Technically, Dietrich could not even visit his parents, who had now moved to the suburb of Charlottenburg, but he did anyway. During one of these trips, early in 1938, Dietrich was arrested at a small meeting of clergymen in Berlin, jailed for the day, put back on a train to Schlawe, and warned not to return. He continued to visit his parents, but he no longer attended conferences. His brother-in-law Hans von Dohnanyi kept him well informed on everything that was happening, especially in the Ministry of Justice. Between the brothers and the brothers-in-law, the Bonhoeffers had access to information from every department of government and even from the Nazi party.

However great the pressure against the Confessing Church, the pressure against the Jews was even greater. Those in the civil service, in teaching, and in medicine lost their jobs. Their passports were stamped with a red "J" for *Jude*. To stop Jews from fleeing, their bank accounts were frozen. There was even talk of sealing the borders. One November day in 1937, Dietrich piled into his Mercedes, inviting Eberhard Bethge along, and headed for Göttingen to visit his twin, Sabine. Her husband, Gerhard Leibholz, was Jewish, a professor of law, and Dietrich was genuinely concerned for their safety.

The four adults plotted an elaborate escape without telling the children or the servants. Trying to look like tourists, they headed off in two cars for the Swiss border as if they were off on a holiday. The only giveaway to the two little girls was that they both wore a double set of clothes to have something extra to wear after the escape. They crossed the Swiss border in the middle of the night with no trouble at the frontier. As the anti-Semitic pressures worsened, phone calls from the family in Berlin suggested the Leibholzes either remain in Switzerland or make their way to England.

In November 1937 through 1938, the Nazi timetable moved into high gear. All young men were required to register for the draft. Czechoslovakia was threatened. The party gave the order for "Crystal Night," when the *gauleiters* burned down Jewish synagogues, businesses, and homes. In Outer Pomerania, Dietrich quietly preached to his students on Psalm 74, "They have burned up all the synagogues of God in the land." He said the target next time would be churches, not synagogues.

In Berlin, the new measures brought on a strong surge of resistance to Allied domination. A year earlier, Hitler had made a solemn and secret presentation to the General Staff. He argued that every generation needed a war. He said that Germany needed to win back the territories stolen from her at Versailles after World War I and would get them either by peaceful means or by war. In the *Reichskanzlei* and in the *Obersalzberg*, Hitler had worked out plans for full-scale war.

The opposition was also at work. Ludwig Beck, chief of the General Staff, like almost every other ranking officer of the military services, thought Hitler crazy. Beck could not control the Gestapo, the political side of the secret service, but he could control the Abwehr, the military side. And the Abwehr had its own intelligence, political as well as military.

Hitler's first step was to recover the German-speaking area of Czechoslovakia, the Sudetenland, which had been taken from Germany at the Treaty of Versailles. The code name for this project was "Operation Green." Ludwig Beck thought an armed attack against Czechoslovakia was an overt act of war. Immediately before the scheduled date of "Operation Green," Beck and other senior officers of the General Staff planned to stage a military *putsch*, kick Hitler out of office, and establish a military government. With Hitler's popularity at low ebb, Beck's plan did not seem unreasonable. The church, the universities, the business world, the Jews, and the newspapers obviously would side with the General Staff. Admiral Walter Canaris, chief of the Abwehr, and its second in command, General Hans Oster, made standby plans to assassinate the *Führer*.

The plotting began late in 1937 and continued throughout 1938, infiltrating several of the Reich ministries. Hans von Dohnanyi served as Oster's contact man and used his cool and calm intelligence as Admiral Canaris's confidential aide. A master plotter, lawyer von Dohnanyi maintained a legal transcript outlining all the Nazi transgressions for future evidence in a court of law.

The circle of friends and relatives around the Bonhoeffer home, now on the Marienburgerallee, was all deeply involved in the plotting. Dr. Karl Bonhoeffer and his friends gathered Hitler's medical and psychiatric records, convinced they could make a strong case against his sanity. Should there be a *putsch,* such evidence would be useful in the winning of the people.

At this stage of the game, Dietrich knew only a little of what was happening. There was no doubt about his loyalty or his ability to keep a secret, but he had no need to know—he was still in Pomerania training ordinands. Hans did ask some odd questions, almost all of them about the moral dimensions of the Christian faith. What did Christ mean when He said that those who take the sword shall also perish by the sword? In ordinary times, that question might have been innocent. Was it so innocent now? Hans clearly had tipped his hand.

The fanciful plot to kill Hitler never had a chance to develop. To get back the lost Sudetenland, the *Führer* worked on England, and he proved a far better bluffer and negotiator than anyone imagined. For preliminary discussions, the diplomats were flying back and forth across the English Channel. Meanwhile, General Ludwig Beck and the General Staff continued to plot against Hitler. They scheduled their *putsch* for September 30, 1938, immediately before "Operation Green."

Then came the bombshell. Neville Chamberlain, prime minister of Britain, flew to Munich on an appeasement mission. Using the slogan of "peace in our time," he agreed to return to Germany those sections of Czechoslovakia that had been taken away by the Treaty of Versailles. Hitler did not even stay in Berlin. He flew to his mountain retreat to celebrate. In the heavily guarded fortress of the *Obersalzberg*, an attempt at assassination was almost out of the question. Now Hitler was both master of Czechoslovakia and a popular hero. The chance for a successful revolt had passed.

21

Clouds of Doubt

The clouds of war in Europe continued to gather, casting an ever more ominous shadow. Dietrich felt as if he were locked into a suit of armor, unable to escape. As a pastor of the Confessing Church, now illegal, he had absolutely no leverage. What should he do? The students at Köslin and Sigurdshof still offered him considerable challenge, though there was no longer any place they could serve, once graduated. Any month now they and he would all be drafted.

By the spring of 1939, Dietrich felt more and more useless, struggling helplessly against the Nazi dragon. He found life increasingly complicated. Because they could not legally travel to visit one another, the Bonhoeffer family invented code words for their letters and telephone calls. "Onkel Rudi" meant the war they were all sure of was not far away. Meanwhile, Dietrich left for England to see Sabine and bring her word of the family. An additional purpose was to seek the counsel of Bishop Bell and to bring him up-to-date on the church struggle.

From Bell, Dietrich received the advice he needed. Bell suggested he should not throw himself away needlessly but husband his talents for something truly significant. There was no need to feel guilty or heroic. Why not remain in England and serve a German parish, as he had done before? Dietrich said he felt he was not really cut out for congregational work. Besides, German citizens living in England probably would be interned if war came.

Bell also talked of an appointment in Geneva with the World Alliance of Churches. In fact, Dietrich spent several challenging hours with Willem Visser't Hooft, the young Dutchman who was in the process of changing the World Alliance of Churches into the World Council of Churches. After Dietrich's competent work at the conferences, the staff would certainly welcome him. The trouble was that with the Confessing Church outlawed, he did not really represent any church. Naturally, Bishop Heckel could be expected to raise strong objections. Besides, the most influential man on the World Alliance was no longer Bishop Bell but Archbishop William Temple, who did not know Bonhoeffer well.

There was yet a third possibility: the United States. Reinhold Niebuhr was shortly to present a series of lectures in Scotland and was vacationing at a small village in Surrey. Dietrich drove down to talk over the old school days at Union. The scene of their chat was an enchanting English garden of boxwood and daffodils. Niebuhr saw no problem in finding Dietrich a job. What did Bonhoeffer want to do? Teach? Run a parish? Lecture? Dietrich was genuinely confused and hopelessly indecisive. He did not want to stay in Germany and end up a dead infantryman like his brother Walter in World War I. He saw little chance of carrying on any real kind of ministry in Nazi Germany. But he did not know what he really wanted.

Niebuhr responded with quick letters to America. Henry Smith Leiper, head of the National Council of Churches, arranged a summer lectureship at Union, then a job in New York as pastor to the horde of refugees streaming in from Germany. In the Midwest, Paul Lehmann, the graduate assistant who had befriended Dietrich at Union, already had begun scheduling a series of lectures so Dietrich could combine his two loves: theology and travel.

Early in June, only a week or two ahead of the draft in Germany, Dietrich and his oldest brother, Karl-Friedrich, sailed from Southampton. Karl was scheduled for a summer lectureship at the University of Chicago. In the daily routine aboard ship, Bonhoeffer rediscovered a calm of the soul he had long missed. Like his mother, he always had read the *Losungen*, a series of daily Bible meditations published by the Moravian Brethren. These helped him see himself once again as a humble believer. Dietrich was only 32, with a sound theological background, of considerable value to any church. How could he use his talents most effectively? Was he only running away again?

In New York, Dietrich received a hero's welcome, with Henry Smith Leiper present to cart him off the boat and an invitation to stay at the Connecticut home of Dr. Henry Sloane Coffin, the president of Union Theological Seminary. Dietrich thought clearly, talked forcefully, and ate well. His return revived old friendships with those he had known eight years earlier. He was excited about the possibility of a staff job with the Student Christian Movement that would include teaching and the lecture circuit. Yet an increasing cloud of doubt darkened his eagerness. Those meditations from the Moravians were working at his soul. Should he return to Germany? He did not want to be a pastor to refugees for fear the Nazis would never let him return to his homeland in case they won the war.

For once Dietrich made up his mind quickly. If war broke out, he did not want to be caught in the United States. That would probably mean internment if the Americans were involved. Only two months earlier, by contrast, he had suggested he would not mind being caught in England with Sabine. Now Dietrich felt his place was in Germany, with the people of his birth. He read the mail from home and anxiously inquired when his father thought "Onkel Rudi" would arrive.

Dietrich regretfully wrote Paul Lehmann in Chicago that the lecture circuit would have to go by the board. Paul was not convinced. He traveled to New York to persuade Dietrich to sit out the war in safety and save himself for the rebuilding of Germany afterward. Instead, he arrived only to wave Dietrich off at the docks.

Dietrich's decision was now cast in concrete. He wrote Niebuhr, who had been extremely kind in making these now useless arrangements:

> I have come to the conclusion that I made a mistake in coming to America. I must live through this difficult period of our national history with the Christian people of Germany. I will not have the right to participate in the reconstruction of Christian life in Germany after the war if I do not share the trials of this time with my people.

Dietrich usually had trouble reaching and sticking with a decision. Making so important a choice in New York, where he did not feel at home, was doubly difficult. One consideration was the

Leibholzes, his sister Sabine and her family, whom he had hoped to bring to America once he got settled, especially if the United States did not enter the war. Doubtless his decision also involved his reactions toward the American religious scene: He did not understand it, he did not trust it, he did not like it. In less than 30 days, Dietrich had dropped anchor in New York, changed his mind, and was now sailing for Europe again. On the return journey, he stayed in England with Sabine for two weeks, not like the five in March and April, anxious lest "Onkel Rudi" overtake him.

In Berlin, the summer of 1939 had been in some ways quieter than the one in New York. Dietrich was no more missed than if he had gone off on a holiday to Spain or Italy. He joined his House of Brothers at the beach, those who were not yet drafted, and heard of the peace pact between Germany and Russia. He applied for a job as a military chaplain. The *vikariat* kept him occupied until it was finally closed half a year later.

On September 1, 1939, the roar of dive-bombing Stukas over the plains of Poland demonstrated that "Onkel Rudi" had in fact arrived. Two days later, Great Britain responded with a declaration of war, and World War II had begun. At the delightful hunting lodge at Sigurdshof, Dietrich was too far from Berlin to stay abreast of the latest news, but the rumble of tanks through Pomerania already was changing his whole way of life.

Dietrich had begun writing another book, *Ethics,* and had been rethinking what a Christian's responsibilities really were when his life switched from one of peaceful reverie to one of drastic atrocity. In his book, he saw quite clearly that man is no simple mixture of good and evil. By nature, he is both. "Shakespeare's characters now walk in our midst," Dietrich wrote, "both the villain and the saint." He recognized that even a man of God like himself might have to assume some degree of evil to achieve a greater good, hate it as he might.

Dietrich did not want to be thought radical. What one does must always be well thought out, well prepared, logical. It must have an ethical purpose. There is no point in trading in a "rusty sword" for a burnished one if all one plans to do is wave it aimlessly in the air.

By the end of September, the German tanks and dive-bombers had wiped out Poland. Germany buzzed with rumors of atrocities committed by the troops of the SS (the *Schutzstaffel* or

"protecting shield"), often at the insistence of Nazi political officers. Most Germans rejoiced at the quick victory, finally getting
some revenge for the Treaty of Versailles. Yet the bloodthirstiness
of the attack and the use of dive-bombers and tanks against
unarmed villagers was disturbing. The intellectuals who had
opposed Hitler in time of peace opposed him even more in time of
war, though now their objections had to be more guarded.

Dietrich occasionally caught the train to Berlin to visit his
parents. Although not directly involved in the conspiracy against
Hitler, he did have some inkling of what was happening. Often he
served as a kind of conscience to the various plotters, especially for
his brothers-in-law Hans von Dohnanyi and Rüdiger Schleicher.
The planning centered in the offices of General Ludwig von Beck
and in those of the Abwehr, made up mainly of high-ranking officers of the General Staff, the elite of the military machine. To provide civilian input, there also were administrators from the civil
service, as well as lawyers and professional men.

Another group of conspirators that opposed both the
blitzkrieg and the Nazi philosophy was the Kreisau Circle, which
met regularly at the country home of Helmuth von Moltke. The
group included Peter Count York and Adam von Trott. All three
were young lawyers and noblemen. Without an army under its
command, however, the Kreisau Circle was not as potentially dangerous to Hitler as the Abwehr. The Kreisau nobles concerned
themselves more with Germany's future, if Hitler should fall or be
assassinated, than how to do away with him. Yet throughout the
war, the two groups kept close contact with each other. Other
groups and individuals also worked for an end to hostilities or an
end to Hitler.

So far the only military action had been in Poland, and that
was now over. At the highest levels of world government, especially in England and America, there was continuing hope that
peace might still be arbitrated. Payne Best, a young captain in the
British intelligence and a man who was present when Bonhoeffer
died, was captured that autumn on the Dutch border. He had been
trying to contact the German underground and test the mood for
an armistice. Other hopes for peace were being nursed at the
World Council of Churches and at the Vatican.

Hitler was not wholly unaware of the plots against him. He
was almost superstitiously suspicious of the military, especially of

the Old Guard. To counteract the Abwehr and to backstop the Gestapo, he established a third security arm, the *Reichssicherheits-hauptamt,* the Reich Security Head Office, usually abbreviated to RSHA. Whether he was in the chancellery at Berlin, in the Berghof, in the Eagle's Nest, or in the Wolf's Lair, Hitler took special care to surround himself with loyal bodyguards.

Dietrich expected to be drafted into the army, along with his seven remaining students, at any moment. However, the war had turned sleepy, with more planning than fighting. Not until the following April did it revive. Meanwhile, through his family, Dietrich inquired about a military chaplaincy. He did not go through the usual channels, which would mean applying to the consistory of the *Reichskirche.* To him this would have been knuckling under. In any case, he was too late—the army was now accepting only those with previous military experience.

In the spring, Hitler's dive-bombers and panzers again came alive. In April he swallowed up Denmark and Norway. In May he took Holland, Belgium, and Luxemburg. In June he sliced through France to the English Channel, and France promptly capitulated. Hitler now controlled an empire the size of Napoleon's and faced the enormous task of consolidating his conquests into a mighty fortress, a *Festung Europa.* The surprisingly quick victory over France won Hitler the immediate plaudits of his people, who had too long played poor brothers to the French and the British.

The night Paris fell in June 1940, Bonhoeffer and Bethge were preaching in the German city of Memel in what was once Lithuania. The previous night, Stalin had borrowed a page from Hitler, announcing his plan to invade Latvia, Lithuania, and Estonia. Out on the Baltic, the German navy was laying mines and cleaning gun turrets, eager to slow Russia down. Over the loudspeakers in the cafe came the announcement that France had surrendered.

The townsfolk danced for joy and sang "Deutschland über Alles," the national anthem. Up and down the streets, there was the exchanging of the Hitler salute, the *sieg heil.* Dietrich also rose and saluted, a little to the chagrin of his younger friend Eberhard. "Raise your arm," Dietrich whispered. "Are you crazy? We shall have to run risks for very different things now, but not for that salute."

22

Traveling Negotiator

The collapse of France and the encirclement of the British army at Dunkirk in June 1940 gave the war a whole new face. Hitler now controlled the heartland of Europe, with its mines, factories, and refineries. Atrocities multiplied. The imprisonment of those who opposed the regime steadily increased, and the shunting of Jews into the concentration camps began to pick up speed. The party was now stressing the eugenics laws. Waves of "mercy killings" began to thin the ranks of the mentally retarded, the epileptics, the aged, and all those who could not actively work.

With the *Sammelvikariat* now ended, Dietrich made the Kleist estate at Klein Krossin his headquarters. Increasingly, he found himself under police surveillance. Several times they interrupted his services or meetings. Dietrich returned to Berlin to discuss his problems with Hans von Dohnanyi and his friends. To them the answer was simple. They named Dietrich a special investigator for the secret service. As one who bore *V-mann* credentials from the Abwehr, the Gestapo could no longer interfere with his travel.

The Gestapo quickly retaliated. Because Dietrich was still a member of the Confessing Church, they officially declared him a member of an illegal organization and, therefore, an enemy of the state. Dietrich could no longer preach or make speeches. He found himself under almost constant surveillance. The Abwehr then posted him to Munich to confer with Joseph Müller, the Catholic lawyer who had been conducting secret negotiations with the Vatican.

Dietrich planned to live at the summer home of a fellow theologian, Gerhard von Rad, on the Chiemsee, but Müller found him even more comfortable accommodations at the pleasant old Benedictine abbey at Ettal. There he would not have the bother of cooking his own meals or washing his dishes, and he would have a comfortable bed, a fine library, and good care. For someone with Dietrich's habits, smoking pack after pack of cigarettes, reading all through the night, somewhat detached from housekeeping, the monastery was a wise choice.

For six months, Dietrich lived an ideal life. He had been forbidden to publish, but he still worked away at the *Ethics* manuscript. He took a break now and then by skiing or tramping through the snow. Down the road from the abbey was the magnificent Linderhof, the summer palace of the mad King Ludwig, and for additional diversion, the mountain village of Oberammergau, famous for its Passion Play, was nearby.

Occasionally, Dietrich traveled to Berlin or to Klein Krossin. By the spring of 1941, the war began to look somewhat more promising to the plotters of the Abwehr and those of the Kreisau Circle. Hitler was not invincible. The Luftwaffe's attack on Great Britain did not succeed, and waves of Spitfires fought off the bombers, prompting Winston Churchill to say, "Never in the field of human endeavor was so much owed by so many to so few."

In America, Roosevelt had been elected to a third term, and though the Japanese would not attack Pearl Harbor until six months later, prompting the United States to enter the war, American public opinion was swinging rapidly against the Nazis. In Greece, the forces of Mussolini were stopped, and even the massive panzer divisions of the Germans thought twice about confronting the manpower of Russia.

Ludwig von Beck, chief of staff for the armed forces, resigned, totally unable to stomach Hitler's atrocities. With Beck went the best chance for a military *putsch*. His replacement, Walther von Brauchitsch, knew that all talk of revolt was treasonable and did not want to be implicated.

Meanwhile, Dietrich was off on the first of three wartime trips to Geneva. From the Germans there, both with the World Council of Churches and with the International Red Cross, he learned that England might still be willing to negotiate. Winston Churchill was now prime minister, however, and insisted on unconditional surrender.

Dietrich stayed nearly a month, visiting both Erwin Sutz and Karl Barth. Barth could still not figure out what Dietrich's mission was or why he was traveling on behalf of the German Secret Service. Even in Geneva, there was speculation about whom Dietrich really represented and where his loyalties lay. Of his old friends, Willem Visser't Hooft was one of the few to accept Dietrich at face value and to appreciate how considerable the opposition to Hitler really was. Visser't Hooft relayed this information to Bishop Bell in England, but again he raised the problem that bothered all the plotters. If Hitler were assassinated, would he be considered a martyr? Would an even worse demagogue replace him?

From Geneva, Dietrich returned not to Ettal or Munich, but to Berlin. There he took a personal interest in a new Abwehr project. Jews were now required to wear on their clothes the yellow Star of David. The experimental programs of "elimination" and "liquidation" were no longer experimental; they were policy. Canaris and Dohnanyi had Jewish friends of long standing they wanted to smuggle to Switzerland, ostensibly as agents of the secret service. Originally, seven people were involved, providing the code name U-7.

Providing safe conduct passes was no problem. These the Abwehr could issue. The real difficulty lay with the other ministries: labor, finance, foreign office, and banking. An enormous amount of subterfuge and manipulation was involved, including some personal dickering with the dreaded Reich Security Head Office. Eventually the operation was a great success, though it provided evidence that would later be used at the court-martials of Canaris, Dohnanyi, and Bonhoeffer.

In September 1941, Dietrich made a second journey to Geneva. This time he was accompanied by General Thomas, Quartermaster General of the German forces. Thomas's job was to establish communications and supply networks that might be useful in case of a *putsch*. Dietrich's conferences with Visser't Hooft reinforced the hopes of the German underground for a negotiated peace.

In the spring of 1942, German forces in Norway stirred up a hornets' nest. Vidkun Quisling, the Norwegian collaborator, locked Dean Arne Fjellbu of Trondheim out of his cathedral. Quisling ordered all youth groups into the *Hitlerjugend*, causing a general strike. To Dietrich, this was an exciting development. Years earlier he had unsuccessfully advocated a similar strike among the clergy in Germany. In Norway, the plan seemed to be working.

Because the troubles in Norway were church-related, the Abwehr had good reason to send a pair of religiously oriented advisers, Count Helmuth von Moltke, head of the Kreisau Circle, and Dietrich Bonhoeffer. Despite the Abwehr cover, Dietrich felt as if he were continually being watched. He and von Moltke made the rounds of churchmen and military governors. They secretly encouraged the pastors to continue the strike and the governors not to be so adamant. From Berlin, Martin Bormann approved the proposed compromise. Bishop Eivind Berggrav could be released from custody, though he would have to live outside Oslo. Dean Fjellbu could go back to his pulpit at Trondheim. Under these terms, the Nazi overlords and the Norwegian patriots reached a shaky settlement.

Dietrich's third wartime visit to Switzerland came in May 1942. This was no leisurely tour of lakeside homes where he could work at another chapter of the *Ethics* and play. The two men he wanted most to see, Willem Visser't Hooft and Hans Schönfeld, both were gone. General Secretary Visser't Hooft had flown to England via Spain, and Head of Research Schönfeld was in Stockholm to meet Bishop George Bell. Almost at once, Dietrich decided to break off the visit to Geneva and leave for Stockholm. He was quite certain he could arrange the travel papers through the Abwehr. Furthermore, he doubted Schönfeld's competence to negotiate with the English peace groups, though that was the job with which Visser't Hooft and the World Council had charged him.

After a quick stop in Berlin, Dietrich took what for him was a rather drastic step. He flew to Stockholm. Normally, he hated aircraft and became airsick, but this was something of an emergency. He found the conferees in Sigtuna at an evangelical academy. Obviously, Bishop Bell was delighted not only to be meeting with the official party from Geneva, but also to see his old friend of London days.

Privately, Bonhoeffer could provide what the official commissioners could not: an up-to-date report from the highest circles of Berlin, even the names of the conspirators. These included the ranking field marshals, colonel-generals, and chiefs of staff of the Wehrmacht: von Beck, Gordeler, von Hammerstein, Schacht, Bock, Kluge, and Leuschner. Bell advised extreme caution. Although his contacts with Anthony Eden and with the American ambassador John Winant were quite solid, those with Churchill were not. He could promise nothing, even if Hitler were assassinated. Yet he would gladly relay any proposals.

Schönfeld's information seems to have originated with the Kreisau Circle and Bonhoeffer's with the Abwehr. For Bishop Bell to sort out the two schemes may have provided difficulty, but to have two points of view also gave depth. The range of discussion was as broad as one might have expected of diplomats rather than churchmen: restoration of the monarchy, overthrow of the Nazis, takeover of the *Schutzstaffel*, arrangements for secret messages, and recovery of a token colony or two.

When he returned to London, Bishop Bell made a valiant effort to win the conspirators a hearing. The ground already had been prepared by Willem Visser't Hooft and Adam von Trott, who had just left. Yet in the eyes of the Western leaders, the war seemed to have gone past the point of peace-feelers. Bell wrote his findings in a report to the British cabinet. He was received with great kindness, both by Anthony Eden and Sir Stafford Cripps. Winant immediately forwarded copies of the documents to Washington.

But the timing was bad. This was June 1942, only seven months after Japan had bombed Pearl Harbor. The United States was gearing up for war, and German bombs that cried out for vengeance were still smashing Britain. For the first time, Hitler's tanks had been slowed by a horrible Russian winter that kept them immobile for five months. Washington and London agreed that any *putsch* against Hitler would be welcome. Yet they demanded not only unconditional surrender, but punishment of the German people. Louis Lochner, a noted American journalist who returned to Washington from Berlin the same month Dietrich visited Sigtuna, could get no presidential response when he talked about the high-ranking Germans who, at considerable risk to their own lives, still actively opposed the Nazi regime.

June 1942 was a busy month for Dietrich. He already had been to Switzerland and Sweden. Now he was off to Italy. He began to enjoy the busy life of a *V-mann*, especially the chance to travel. Dohnanyi originated the trip to Venice. Dietrich went along as a German churchman of note to help set a good tone in dealing with the Catholic hierarchy. The contact there for the underground was Wilhelm Schmidhuber, a German businessman who frequently passed money and information to opposition groups in the Balkans.

After talking to Schmidhuber, Dietrich dreamed up a grand scheme that would send him scurrying to Hungary, Bulgaria, Greece, Turkey, and Croatia. Even with the protection of the Abwehr, he would need a perfect cover story. The Gestapo and the RSHA were growing increasingly suspicious. What prevented the trip was the Gestapo's arrest of Schmidhuber. With him in a con-centration camp, Dietrich no longer had access to the valuable list of agents and contacts, or any channels to smuggle money, and his scheme of playing agent provocateur in the Balkans collapsed.

23

Falling in Love

During the busy month of June 1942, after Dietrich's trips to Switzerland and Sweden and before the one to Italy, he stopped again at his favorite country house, Klein Krossin, to visit the elderly duchess he called his "grandmother," Frau Ruth von Kleist-Retzow. Perhaps the quarter of his blood that was Pomeranian made him feel more at home in the lush forests and meadows of the Junkers than anywhere else in the world. Perhaps the drawing card was his benefactress. She was pious, generous, intelligent, cultured, hardworking, and strong-willed.

In summer, the manor house was full of grandchildren. From his perch at the grand piano or at the writing desk, Dietrich was quick to notice the adoring eyes and gracious manners of one of those granddaughters, Maria von Wedemeyer. Maria was one of seven children of Max von Wedemeyer. Six years earlier, her grandmother had brought her to Finkenwalde for confirmation instruction, but the teacher—Dietrich—had said she was too young.

Now, at a beautiful 18, she could not avoid notice. Poised, fresh, cultured, filled with vitality, she was the image of everything Dietrich would have longed for in a wife. She was 17 years younger than he, but nonetheless he fell head over heels in love. So did she. Dietrich always had thought of himself as intellectual and rational, but now he was pleased to discover in himself genuine emotion. In less than a week, his world had taken on a whole new dimension. He was in love.

Dietrich was also cautious and realistic. He feared he was far too old and bachelorized for her. Yet marriage had not been altogether remote from his thinking. Almost every month he preached at the wedding of one of his seminarians. Erwin Sutz, Dietrich's Swiss friend of about the same age, had married recently. On a visit, Dietrich envied the newlyweds their happiness. Maria's father, Max, was an officer stationed at the Russian front. A strong supporter of the Confessing Church and an active politician, he died under a Russian artillery barrage two months later. Dietrich immediately wrote the widow a letter of condolence, but there was not one word about Maria.

Still, the romance continued to grow. Maria and Dietrich saw each other occasionally during the autumn of 1942 at Klein Krossin or in Berlin when she came to see a play or an opera. Dietrich did not yet want to tell his parents of his romantic interests, but he had to tell somebody, so he told Eberhard Bethge. Bethge was having a similar problem. He was also in love with a girl too young: Dietrich's niece and godchild, the daughter of the Schleichers.

Maria's mother had seen many wartime romances and was reluctant to let an 18-year-old, no matter how mature she seemed, make her own decision. Frau von Wedemeyer had not seen Dietrich nearly as often as had her mother or daughter. Besides, the whole family had not yet begun to recover from her husband's death. Then there was the question of Bonhoeffer's political shenanigans. She knew he had no "official" position or congregation, so what did he really do? Work for Hitler?

At the end of November, Maria's mother invited Dietrich to the von Wedemeyer home at Patzig. Dietrich did not know what to expect, but he did know that both he and Maria cared for each other and that it was past time to involve her mother. The welcome was not as warm as he had hoped. Maria, said her mother, was still young and emotionally bothered by the death of her father. Could they not agree to separate for a year and make certain of their feelings?

Although Dietrich always had been close to his own mother, he could not gather the courage to talk to her about Maria. Was Frau von Wedemeyer right? Was the whole romance crazy, a man of 37 marrying a girl of 18? The year's ban did not last. Maria's feelings were far too strong. She worked at her mother almost constantly, and at her guardian as well. Two months later, Maria and Dietrich were engaged. The only victory Frau von Wedemeyer had was a promise to keep the engagement secret.

For the last half of 1942 and the first months of 1943, the plotters of the Abwehr and of the Kreisau Circle found the times more propitious. Hitler's panzers were no longer rolling pell-mell across the plains of Russia, stopped as much by snow and ice as by tanks and guns. In Africa, too, the tide of battle had turned, not because Montgomery was out-generaling Rommel, but because Hitler was now dictating tactics to his field commanders.

Dietrich's continuing friendship with the students from Finkenwalde supplied him with fresh information about the anti-Nazi underground. At one session, the talk turned to what would happen after the war. An old friend from the days of his confirmation class, Hans von Haeften, volunteered that he was now serving as a staff lieutenant at the chancellery. No one paid much attention to how perturbed he was until he blurted out, "Shall I shoot him?" Hans was dead serious. He had almost daily contact with ranking members of the cabinet, including Hitler. He was known and trusted. He saw no difficulty in unholstering his Walther and firing. Yet there was a lingering doubt in his mind. Would it be morally right to shoot Hitler? Was he only trying to seek personal glory, to be a hero?

The group of pastors was shocked and silenced. Dietrich explained that a dead Hitler was not the whole answer. The takeover had to be as carefully prepared as the assassination. Under Himmler or Göring, things might be even worse than under Hitler. The military had to be ready to assume control.

Hans was not satisfied. He came from a noble family that for generations had provided officers for the General Staff. Duty was foremost. The only trouble was his difficulty in identifying where his real duty lay. Should he be an assassin? He and Dietrich talked far into the night. The decision had to be made by Hans and no one else, Dietrich insisted, if he were to live with his conscience afterward. Both knew he would probably not live at all but would himself be shot on the spot. Hans von Haeften left that night still undecided. Later, he did become an aide to Count von Stauffenberg and was deeply involved in the July 20 plot. For that, he was immediately executed without a trial. But that was still 16 months in the future.

Back in 1939, when the war first began, Dietrich would have been shocked at the thought of assassinating anyone. Taught from Luther's catechism, he had been brought up to respect everyone in authority, not only parents and grandparents, but judges, school-masters, the police, and probably even *Führers*. Yet as the atrocities increased—the war casualties, the Jews, the handicapped, the pris-oners of war, the laborers, the underground—he was not so sure.

Of the hundreds of Germans who were involved in plots against Hitler, only a half dozen were clergy. With his pastor friends, Dietrich frequently discussed the right and the wrong of acting against one's *Führer*. One example Dietrich frequently used was that of a crazy drunk driving through the marketplace and running over innocent people. In that kind of situation, what should a Christian do? Only help the injured? Or try to stop the driver?

Inside the Third Reich, there were more and more protests against German atrocities. Much of the information came through the British Broadcasting Corporation's German-language broad-casts. Technically, Germans were not allowed to listen, but their hunger for news that was not controlled by the Nazis was consid-erable. The BBC kept repeating the notion that not all Germans were bad, only those who were around Hitler. This was the stuff of which conspiracies are born. On the other hand, however, Roo-sevelt and Churchill had declared at Casablanca that they would accept nothing but unconditional surrender.

In March 1943, there were two serious attempts on Hitler's life. The code word was "Operation Flash." If Hitler were put out of the way, Oster and Beck had to be absolutely sure the govern-ment would fall into the hands of the General Staff, not into the control of Himmler and Göring. Commanders at Berlin, Vienna, and Munich gave the assurances that once they received the "Flash," they would put the coup into effect.

The *blitzkrieg* had now slowed to the pace of a caterpillar, and on March 13, 1943, Hitler paid a flying visit to his eastern headquarters at Smolensk, deep in Russian territory, to find out what was wrong. There, his host and field commander was Major General Henning von Tresckow. Tresckow's aide was an intimate of Dietrich from the good old days among the Junker families in

Pomerania, Fabian von Schlabrendorff. The plan was simple. With explosives provided by the British underground, von Tresckow and Schlabrendorff would place a bomb aboard the plane returning Hitler to Germany. The package was carried aboard by one of Hitler's unwitting aides. General von Tresckow had told him it was two bottles of brandy he was sending to an old friend for an anniversary.

Once the aircraft soared off the runway, the plotters stood by their phones, waiting for word of the explosion. The first to know would be the fighter planes flying escort. An hour passed, then two, but there was no word. The fuse had been set for 30 minutes. Two and a half hours later, a routine message came through from a refueling stop at Rastenburg. By now the plotters knew something had gone wrong. Von Schlabrendorff set up a special flight to retrieve the unexploded parcel and replace it with one of real brandy. When the bomb was retrieved, he took it apart. The detonator was faulty.

The Abwehr had plenty of agents, and a week later, they geared up for another attempt. The first had apparently gone wholly undetected. The second began in the parlor of the Dohnanyi house in Berlin, and it was there that Hans now waited breathlessly for word of its success. On the surface, the occasion looked like a typical "musical evening." The family was practicing a complicated cantata, "Praise to the Lord, the Almighty," for Dr. Karl Bonhoeffer's 75th birthday.

Dietrich conducted from the piano, Klaus played the cello, and Rudiger the violin. The rest of the family made up the chorus. It was late Sunday afternoon, and Hans waited impatiently for the phone to ring. That morning Hitler was inspecting troops at Smolensk in honor of *Heldengedenktag*, the day Germans remembered the millions who had died in the first World War.

This time the coup was in the hands of a Major von Gersdorff, a staff man attached to the Army Group in Russia. In his pockets, he carried two grenades of English manufacture, their pins ready to pull. This time there would be no faulty detonator. The plan was to show Hitler various kinds of war materiel captured from the Russians. While Gersdorff and Hitler were standing side by side, he would pull the pins. Unfortunately, Hans von Dohnanyi never did receive his phone call that day. Hitler had caught a cold and stuck to his own group. He was not interested in capturing enemy armor, only in winning the war. The MPs kept everyone away from Hitler. An inspection that was scheduled to last 30 minutes took only eight. Gersdorff never got within 20 steps of his victim, and he figured he would have to be within two or three, to make absolutely certain the grenades would be effective.

Again a conspiracy had failed. Dr. Bonhoeffer's birthday party went off on schedule, without interruption. Even Hitler was represented by a man from the Ministry of Culture, awarding the famous psychiatrist the Goethe Medal for Arts and Sciences. The anniversary must have been a little ironic, though, with that representative of the *Reichskanzlei* happily drinking champagne with the Bonhoeffers, unaware that they were a nest of conspirators.

The one consolation to the failed attempt was that the cover for the conspiracy still had not been blown. Admiral Canaris telephoned to say there was no "Flash," but at least the tracks had been covered. The explosives Hans von Dohnanyi had delivered personally to the Eastern front had not succeeded, but neither had they been detected.

24

A Man of Letters

Canaris and Oster had good reason to believe the two attempts they had engineered against Hitler had put no one in real danger. Yet the Gestapo and the RSHA grew increasingly suspicious. A few days after his father's birthday, Dietrich phoned Christel. The voice that answered was that of a stranger. Had Dietrich dialed the wrong number, or was the Gestapo there? He went next door to see Rudi Schleicher.

Late in the afternoon, Dr. Bonhoeffer went next door to tell Dietrich that two men wanted to see him. They were already searching his study but could find nothing incriminating. Nonetheless, they took him away for questioning. They arrested five people that day: Hans Dohnanyi and his wife, Joseph Müller and his wife, and Dietrich.

Müller, the Catholic lawyer from Munich, was the key to the arrests. He and Hans went to the military prison on the Lehrter Strasse under heavy guard, the two women to Charlottenburg, and Dietrich to the rather lenient civil prison at Tegel. No charges were brought against any of the prisoners. The arrests were the result of the illegal money transfers involving Operation U-7. The Gestapo was on a fishing expedition to see what it could catch.

Whether as a free spirit, gourmet, or lover of life, liberty, and the pursuit of success, Dietrich had a difficult time adjusting to prison. There was no Bechstein to play, no fresh strawberries, and certainly no disinfectant to scour the wash basin. There was not even a washbasin. The shock was dramatic, and good writer that he was, he recorded his disgust in notes and letters. A few musty blankets were tossed through the door, but he could not endure their smell and chose instead to shiver. The next morning, the guard tossed a chunk of black bread onto the cement floor. The ersatz coffee was barely warm, with more grounds than liquid.

Dietrich expected the imprisonment to be short, as it had been for many other pastors who had been arrested. He was wrong. He remained in prison for two full years, with 18 months of that time in Tegel. Although he would not have counted the days there as pleasant, neither were they altogether wasted. For once in his life, he had time to sit and think, to meditate, to write, to read. Despite the restrictions, his family and friends found ways to provide books and writing materials, along with food parcels.

If Dietrich's knowledge of the attempts against Hitler had been traceable, he would have been shot at once. Actually there was little hard evidence against him, and what charges there were depended mainly on what could be dug up against Müller and Dohnanyi. More than that, the judicial process involved a dispute over jurisdiction—between the Wehrmacht, on the one side, and the Gestapo and the RSHA, on the other.

The judge who investigated Bonhoeffer was a Nazi party member named Manfred Röder. Röder had made his reputation a year earlier in the prosecution of the "Red Chapel," a communist cell in the Wehrmacht that had plotted to kill Hitler and take over the government. Röder uncovered some 75 plotters in the *Rote Kapelle* and had sentenced all to die.

The case against Bonhoeffer and Dohnanyi was scant. The evidence against them was all carefully buried outside Berlin. Only after the July 20 plot a year later, which rocked Hitler's map room on the Eastern front, was the real truth uncovered. Furthermore, there was built-in protection from the Wehrmacht. Lehmann and Sack were both distinguished attorneys, and they insisted on full compliance with the law, not any stripped-down Gestapo kangaroo court.

The charges against Dietrich were especially thin. For more than half a year, he was investigated but never actually charged. Under German law, he was required to make both spoken and written answers. The investigation involved his connections with the Abwehr and how he could travel and speak wherever he liked, avoiding the Gestapo ban. On that score, he was well covered. Admiral Canaris had ordered him to make the trips. He had not spoken to more than a few people at a time. In his judgment, he was doing his duty to his country, as instructed, serving as pastor of the Confessing Church.

The investigators tried to involve him with the U-7 operation. Dietrich admitted that he might have been a little naive and impulsive, but so early in the war, he saw no harm in helping friends who had previously helped him. As for the currency transactions, they had been approved by the finance ministry, had they not? As for the Jewess Charlotte Friedenthal and her frequent visits to his parents' home, had she not served as his church secretary? Was there anything wrong in helping one's secretary? To the charge that he made frequent trips to Switzerland and Italy, there was fortunately little detail. If his meetings in Geneva, Venice, Basel, and Stockholm had really been investigated, there would have been solid evidence. Röder did not push this issue. Was the idle talk of preachers, even if they came from Switzerland or England or Sweden, all that significant?

Dietrich was also charged with helping his students avoid the draft. Obviously, he had helped them get parishes or chaplaincies and advised them how to deal with their draft boards. Through Dohnanyi, he even got a few of them a job in the Abwehr. But if the intelligence agencies were using Jews and communists, why not use a few student pastors? If there was any doubt about his attitude toward the state, could they not read what he had written in his *Cost of Discipleship*? Had he not personally applied for a chaplaincy?

Through his visitors and the prison staff, Dietrich kept hearing of continuing attempts against Hitler's life. Two, of course, occurred just before he was sent to Tegel in the spring of 1943. There were at least three more that year. One was at a guard tower at the *Führer's* headquarters in East Germany. There, some munitions stored by General Helmuth Stieff exploded prematurely, before Hitler got in range.

Another attempt was by a young lieutenant in the Berghof, part of Hitler's retreat in Berchtesgaden. The officer did get access to the building, but he never got close enough to Hitler to shoot. The third attempt was by another young officer, Axel von dem Bussche, who was modeling a new army overcoat with bombs in each pocket. That one was spoiled by an air raid that sent everyone scurrying for cover.

At first Dietrich's strategy had been to demand an early trial. He was sure he would be acquitted. His legal advisers were not so certain because Röder was a thorough and vindictive prosecutor. The case might even get transferred to a Gestapo court. That would be bad indeed. Dietrich was advised to play for time, in the hope that either Hitler or the Third Reich would come crashing down in flames. The strategy nearly worked. Joseph Müller, the Abwehr agent from Munich, did push for a quick trial, conducting his own defense. The verdict in fact was not guilty. Nevertheless, the Gestapo promptly clapped Müller back into a concentration camp for protective custody.

Dohnanyi's stay at the prison on the Lehrter Strasse was far more difficult. He was already ill and overworked. Varicose veins swelled his legs. In November, his cell took a hit from a British incendiary bomb and he suffered a stroke. He could neither see nor talk. Yet Röder did not let up. He judged Hans sound enough to stand trial. Eventually Dohnanyi felt he could no longer fight. He arranged for the bacteria of scarlet fever and diphtheria to be smuggled into his cell. These brought on paralysis and death.

In the more lenient prison at Tegel, things went better for Dietrich. From his cell on the third floor, he could look out over a park. Beyond was the Borsig locomotive works, a legitimate target for Allied bombers. His cell was primitive, containing only a plank bed, a shelf, a stool, and a toilet bucket. The room was so narrow he could almost reach from wall to wall.

In prison, Dietrich kept even busier than when he was free. He read through the Old Testament at least three times. He found joy in reading everything under the sun. At first he was permitted only one letter every 10 days, all censored by Röder himself, which sometimes caused a month's delay. Soon he found guards who were sympathetic enough to smuggle letters and books in and out. For secret communications with his family, he rigged up a special code. If the book contained a message, incoming or outgoing, the name on the flyleaf was underlined. Starting from the back, he or his parents marked one letter every tenth page.

What made life agreeable was the ready welcome Dietrich found in Tegel. The commandant was an old Wehrmacht type, not a Nazi, and knew well that Dietrich was the nephew of General Paul von Hase, commander of the Berlin district. What the commandant could not legally grant the favored preacher, the guards felt no compunctions about. Quietly they gave him the run of the place. They gave him the chance to talk with his parents, sisters, and fiancée in private when he should have been carefully supervised. They brought him flowers and plants from the prison greenhouse. They circulated the Christmas prayers he wrote. They smuggled out a wedding sermon he wrote when his niece Renate married Eberhard Bethge and another when their first child was born.

The guards took Dietrich to the radio room to listen to the news or to hear Beethoven and Palestrina. They played chess with him. They had him tell their fortunes from their handwriting. They let him use the sick room to write. They sought for him a place of safety during the worst air raids. The commandant could hardly have been ignorant of this special treatment, but he did have to hide these favors when prosecutor Röder visited. After all, Röder had demanded strict isolation of the prisoner.

Once Dietrich was at Tegel, the engagement with Maria von Wedemeyer took on new importance. Her first visit surprised and delighted him. Immediately he fired off to his friends a series of letters about the delights of love, which was quite a switch for a man of 38 who always had thought himself unemotional. In the autumn of 1943, Maria moved to Berlin and stayed with the elder Bonhoeffers. To keep her from being drafted, Dr. Bonhoeffer signed her on as his receptionist.

Although Dietrich found much to keep his mind agile—the Scriptures, meditation, literature, even memorizing the hymns of Paul Gerhardt—the real joy of his life was writing. He tried a variety of genres: fiction, drama, prose, and poetry. He undertook a play, which was not so strange, considering the amateur theatricals he had participated in, or all the Goethe, Schiller, and Lessing he had read. He tried his hand at a novel about a forester and a Pomeranian landholder.

He really came alive in his letters. Of these there was an unending stream. First, he stayed in close contact with Maria. He wrote of her selling the grand piano and buying a smaller one. He thought Maria should buy a cembalo, a small Italian pianoforte. He encouraged her to start her trousseau. His other major correspondents were his parents and Eberhard Bethge. To his parents, he wrote faithfully and frequently, not only about the need for underwear or a sweater, but about all the joys they had brought him as a boy, especially the smell of Christmas candles or the taste of his mother's stollen.

He was perhaps most candid when he wrote Eberhard Bethge, the Saxon who had studied under him at Finkenwalde and become a kind of alter ego. Bethge was now serving with the Wehrmacht in Italy. He was the one man on whom Dietrich could test some of his experimental concepts in theology, a man who would not be shocked and one who could bring out the best in Dietrich. With Niemöller, with Barth, even with Hildebrandt, there was never so much openness. Besides, of those three, two had fled the country and the third was in a concentration camp.

Of the thousands of letters Dietrich wrote from prison, most were destroyed. After the July 20, 1944, plot, family and friends burned everything that might be incriminating, everything that did not bear the stamp of the censor. Yet hundreds of letters did survive, and they make up the bulk of that delightfully human and thoughtful book, *Letters and Papers from Prison*.

In the letters, the real Dietrich Bonhoeffer comes through: the lover of life, the student of nature, the scholar, the traveler, the gourmet, the observer, the dilettante. In them he talks about the delights of a Beethoven concerto, about Karl Barth lighting a cigar as if in the presence of Jehovah, about gathering mushrooms deep in the forest, about the taste of Berlin beer, about the natural course of the church year, and about watching the deer slip out of the forest to feed.

In what he wrote in prison, there was also another element, that of a theologian cut off from his books and dependent on his own intuition. When *Letters and Papers from Prison* first came into print, long after Dietrich's death and long after the war, those who had known him through *The Cost of Discipleship* suddenly discovered a new Bonhoeffer. No longer was he only the pious and zealous disciple. A new note of adaptation to the world had crept in, a practical blending of the inner life of a believer and the outer world of reality.

In any case, the papers from prison reflected a new and experimental outlook. Despite his awesome learning, Dietrich was able to simplify and popularize his thinking. He talked of our natural bent for God by calling the human being *homo religiosus*, a quasi-scientific phrase Bonhoeffer borrowed from the anthropologists. Although religion had often gone astray, he admitted, nevertheless it was a natural "guardian angel of mankind." Our troubles in life he compared to "a sharing in the sufferings of God on earth."

Dietrich used such phrases as "religionless Christianity," "God hypothesis," and "the non-religious interpretation of the Gospel." He called psychology and philosophy the "secular offshoots of Christianity." He objected to preachers "sniffing out people's sins." He summed up all his ideas as a "non-religious interpretation of biblical concepts in a world come of age." Yet this "new" language and insight must be understood in the light of the extraordinary circumstances of the day: Amid social, political, and spiritual chaos in Europe, Dietrich longed to communicate the Gospel in meaningful, relevant ways, especially to agnostics and intellectuals who had dismissed the faith and the church's witness to Christ.

Dietrich's writings from prison revealed a newer and far more practical theologian. For the first time, he was able to look at life from a contemplative perspective and to see what was truly significant and what was not. This is the Dietrich Bonhoeffer who still lives through his writings, even now.

25

The Curtain Falls

In his cell, Dietrich lived from day to day. His life was not unlike that of a monk, though a worldly one. Even a touch of illness was a reminder of his mortality and not to be despised. In some ways, Dietrich enjoyed Tegel. In a simple way, it helped deepen his faith and increased his appreciation for life itself.

On his 38th birthday, February 4, 1944, he was summoned to the visitors' room. Waiting for him was Maria von Wedemeyer. Besides birthday greetings, she brought news of the family. Eberhard Bethge and Renate had had a baby and named it after Onkel Diet. Would he be godfather? In the year since their engagement, Maria had matured quickly and the two were now making marriage plans. What if Dietrich were released? Would he be drafted? Would he be allowed to return to the Confessing Church or the Abwehr? Would there be enough time to marry, or should they wait until after the war?

Inside the books she brought, he deciphered a frightening message, one that was confirmed later in the day by Judge Sack. Admiral Canaris had been betrayed by a defecting agent in Turkey. The whole cover of the Abwehr was blown, and Canaris was fired. The agency was handed over to the RSHA. That could have been a deadly blow, but as the months passed and nothing happened, Dietrich realized that none of the files and records Dohnanyi and the others had carefully hidden had been uncovered. By early summer 1944, there were still hopes of avoiding a trial. The July

20 plot was now well into the planning stage, under the highly capable hands of Count Claus von Stauffenberg. The Allies landed in Normandy in June 1944, aided by Hitler's insistence that the invasion was only a feint.

On June 30, Dietrich played host to his uncle, General Paul von Hase, commandant of Berlin. For five hours, they sat and drank champagne. The general brought details of the July 20 plot, now only weeks away. Despite the careful planning, the *putsch* did not succeed. Hitler, though stunned by the exploding bomb at his headquarters in Ostpreussen, was shielded by a thick oak table. Even worse than the failure to kill him was the plotters' mistaken conviction that they had succeeded, misled by the massive destruction of the building. They flashed the code word throughout the Wehrmacht, thus pointing a finger at all who were involved.

Hitler was not dead. His radio speech to the nation stopped the revolt cold. Von Stauffenberg died immediately before a firing squad, and a tidal wave of arrests swept across *Festung Europa*. The failure had obvious implications for Dietrich Bonhoeffer and Hans von Dohnanyi, even if they already were behind bars. Hitler fumed with anger and at first executed all who might be suspect. Then came a strange cooling of his revenge. Those still alive had to be thoroughly questioned, even tortured, to dig out the roots of the plot.

In a huge hunt for men and documents, the Gestapo discovered a batch of secret papers the Abwehr had buried at Zossen. These included Dohnanyi's chronicles and all the early papers of Canaris and Oster. The game was over. Dohnanyi responded by taking another strain of diphtheria to make himself even sicker. Bonhoeffer put into action a plot to escape. Corporal Knobloch, a friendly guard, would disguise Dietrich in the clothes of an electrician and they would walk out the gate together. He would live in a gardening hut on the outskirts of town. The Schleichers had provided clothes, money, food, and ration books.

Things were happening quickly that first week in October. Hundreds of suspects were hauled off to jail. The Gestapo needed weeks just to round them all up because two-thirds of the addresses in town had been bombed out of existence. A few days before Dietrich's scheduled escape, Klaus was found hiding in the attic of the Schleicher house and was arrested. A day or two later, Schleicher himself was arrested. By now the Bonhoeffer clan had more than its share of jailbirds: Klaus and Dietrich, Schleicher and Dohnanyi. Eberhard Bethge also had been arrested. Now Dietrich was in a quandary. If he fled, he was implying not only his own guilt, but that of his brothers and other family members. But would they not all be shot in a month anyway, as hundreds of others already had been? He could not make up his mind.

The same evidence that pointed an accusing finger at Klaus and Rüdiger also pointed at Dietrich. In the day or two while he was weighing his decision, he was bundled off to the maximum security prison on Prinz Albrecht Strasse, a place no one could walk out of just by donning the coveralls of a workingman.

Prinz Albrecht Strasse was clearly a jail much worse than Tegel. With a group of other high-ranking prisoners, Dietrich lived below ground in a cell scarcely five feet by eight. There was no window for air or light, only a table, a stool, and a cot. The easygoing days of smuggled letters and books were past, though now and then one of the guards was good enough to deliver a food package from Maria or his parents.

Here life was an endless treadmill of brown bread, thin soup, weak coffee, dank walls, and interrogations. The jail had no exercise yard, and what little movement the prisoners got was walking up and down the corridor, as dark and dank as their cells. At one end were showers, exhilaratingly cold but at least a place where one had the chance to talk to the other prisoners.

The whole hierarchy of the Abwehr was there: Canaris, Oster, Müller, Gordeler, Schlabrendorff, and a dozen others Dietrich did not even know were involved. What any of them got from home they shared: food, cigars, books, and writing paper. The frequent air raids were welcome, providing a chance to exchange news during the prisoner transfers and maybe even a chance to escape.

The four months Dietrich spent at Prinz Albrecht Strasse during the winter of 1944–45 were grim, both for him and for Nazi Germany. Russia was slamming hard against the Eastern front and the Allies against the west. What had only a year or two earlier been an empire bigger than Napoleon's, now began to look as small as the old kingdoms of Prussia and Bavaria. People froze, went hungry, and wore old clothes. The daily rain of bombs killed tens of thousands.

In January 1945, Ruth von Wedemeyer asked her daughter Maria to make a quick trip home, hitch up a wagon, and drive her brothers and sisters westward to Celle. Russian shells were crashing toward the family estate, and in fact before the week was out, all Patzig and the manor house lay in rubble and ashes. In weather that hovered only a few degrees above zero, Maria delivered the children safely.

Back in Berlin at the beginning of February, Maria discovered that her fiancé was no longer at Prinz Albrecht Strasse. In fact, the prison had taken so many hits from high explosives that half the walls had collapsed. Prisoners who were not already under a death sentence were loaded into trucks and hauled to the concentration camp at Buchenwald. Despite continuing queries, neither Maria nor the Bonhoeffer parents could learn Dietrich's whereabouts, or even if he were still alive. For more than a month, Maria wandered between Sachsenhausen, Buchenwald, Dachau, and Flossenbürg, hopeful of finding Dietrich, always carrying a satchel of warm clothing and food.

At Buchenwald, the cells for the 20 high-ranking prisoners such as Dietrich lay just outside the camp in a former air raid shelter. Of all the prisons where Dietrich had stayed, this was the dankest and gloomiest. Fortunately his stay was short. By Easter, April 1, the rumble of American artillery west of the river echoed inside the masonry of the bunkers.

Late on Easter Tuesday, with the Americans about to overrun Buchenwald, the prisoners were loaded aboard a truck that was headed for Flossenbürg. The mere name of Flossenbürg aroused fear. Everybody knew it was an extermination camp. By dawn, the truck reached the turn to head up the valley. From inside the truck, one could hear the roar of motorcycles and garbled conversation. The couriers called out three names, including Müller and Liedig. Gehre, a friend of Müller, also jumped out. Apparently the guards were tired and confused. They wanted three men and got three. They mistook Gehre for Bonhoeffer.

From there, the van plodded on toward Regensburg, arriving at midnight. The prisoners slept in an old barracks, in the same building as the families of some of Germany's most distinguished generals. The next evening, Thursday of Easter week, the guards again herded their prisoners aboard the smoky charcoal-burner. This time the truck broke down along the road, and they sat all night awaiting transport. Finally, a bus showed up. By now prisoners and guards were in such a good mood, intoxicated by the smells of a Bavarian spring, they pretended to be a film company when questioned by some of the girls of the village who were begging for a ride.

Their new destination was a school in the village of Schönberg. The prisons were all full. To Dietrich, there was a sense of relief in finding himself a hundred miles from Flossenbürg, high up in the Bohemian Forest on the mountainous border of Germany and Czechoslovakia. The schoolroom made a beautiful jail, with comfortable beds, clean curtains, and brilliant sunshine. This was rural Oberbayern at its best. The villagers brought in food— food not so easily obtainable in Berlin. Shortly after arriving, the prisoners were joined by the political families they had bumped into at Regensburg.

Despite the sunshine, April 5 proved to be a gloomy day for Bonhoeffer. In Berlin, amid a rain of bombs, Adolf Hitler had just read the secret diaries of Admiral Walter Canaris. These clearly listed plots and plotters. Although Hitler would take his own life two weeks later, he wanted none of those who had plotted against him to live. The day of his decision was Thursday, April 5, 1945. He was still enough of a German and a believer in law and order to hold formal trials. For the "special prisoners" at Flossenbürg, he dispatched one judge from Berlin and another from Nürnberg to give the death warrants the stamp of legality.

On Sunday morning, April 8, 1945, everything was set for the final court-martial at Flossenbürg. The two judges arrived, almost miraculously. One had been strafed from the air in his car and the other had had a train blown up beneath him. Prisoners Canaris, Oster, Sack, Strünck, and Gehre were all present and accounted for. But what about Bonhoeffer? What had happened to Dietrich Bonhoeffer? Had he escaped?

After some frantic telephone calls, the guards were overjoyed to discover that Dietrich had not really escaped, but had merely been misplaced. Yet Schönberg was more than a hundred miles away, over a twisting mountain road. Ordinarily, they would not have had enough gasoline to get him, but these orders came from the *Führer*.

In the beauty of a Bavarian spring, Dietrich had been conducting a service for his fellow prisoners. The Sunday was *Quasi-*

modogeniti, the first Latin word for one of the appointed Scripture readings: "As new born babes, desire the sincere milk of the Word." Dietrich spoke simply and informally. In the adjoining room, the other prisoners schemed how they could smuggle him through the locked door to conduct a second service. At that point, the guards arrived and ordered Dietrich to gather his belongings and accompany them. Bonhoeffer paused to write a message in one of his books, with the request that it be passed on to his parents. He asked Payne Best, a British intelligence agent and fellow prisoner, who later wrote at length about the incidents at Buchenwald and Schönberg, to remember him to Bishop George Bell of Chichester.

The trials must have been nearly completed by the time Dietrich reached Flossenbürg. Each of the accused faced the court-martial individually, though with the documents from Zossen and with Canaris's diary for evidence, the hearings were a mere formality. The courtroom, ordinarily the bakehouse, smelled of warm bread. Bonhoeffer must have arrived about dusk and was the last to be sentenced, perhaps close to midnight.

The hangings took place on the morning of April 9, in the gray light of dawn, on the grounds of the ruined castle. The prison surgeon recorded what happened:

> Between five and six o'clock the prisoners, among them Admiral Canaris, General Oster, ... and Reichsgerichtsrat Sack were taken from their cells and the verdicts of the court martials read out to them. Through the half-open door in one room of the huts I saw Pastor Bonhoeffer, before taking off his prison garb, kneeling on the floor and fervently praying to his God. I was most deeply moved by the way this lovable man prayed, so devout and so certain that God heard his prayer. At the place of execution he again said a short prayer and then climbed the steps to the gallows, brave and composed. His death followed in a few seconds.

26

A Meaningful Life

When April 1945 passed into history, the grand dreams of Adolf Hitler and of Dietrich Bonhoeffer moldered alike under the earth. Bonhoeffer's ashes mingled in a huge mound with those of thousands of others who had passed through the kilns of Flossenbürg, and perhaps even a few who had perished centuries earlier at the hands of the Hohenzollerns, the famous German ruling dynasty. Two weeks later, with Germany in collapse, Hitler wrapped a Walther 7.35 in a towel, put it to his temple, and pulled the trigger. As ordered, his chauffeur poured gasoline over his body and burned it in a bunker under the smashed rose garden of the *Reichskanzlei*.

At Sachsenhausen, Hans von Dohnanyi was executed the same day as Dietrich. Klaus Bonhoeffer and Rudiger Schleicher were shot against the wall of the Lehrter Strasse prison. Since January, Maria von Wedemeyer had been unable to find any trace of her fiancé, but she continued to wander through the ruins of her country, asking anyone who might know of Dietrich's whereabouts. The Russians and Americans were now pounding at the gates of Berlin. With phones, records, mail, and houses hopelessly in shambles, she finally learned of Dietrich's death in June. She could not track down his parents. They heard the news in July when the BBC announced that Bishop George Bell had held a memorial service for Dietrich in London.

The story of Dietrich Bonhoeffer is more than that of a distinguished young man who, like hundreds of others, gave his life in a struggle against the evils of Hitler. In many ways, he typifies the Germany in which he grew up—confused, unstable, searching, restless, dissatisfied. He was always the aristocrat, with all the privileges that class and money could offer in housing, food, cars, and servants. He had the best education his country could provide and had a mind quick to absorb and appreciate all he studied. Despite his gifts, Dietrich was often temperamental. There was nothing that did not excite his interest. He took an almost pagan delight in Goethe, Schiller, and Lessing. He loved the natural world: the heady incense of the fir forests, the exotic aroma of wild strawberries, the mystic twinkle of the Pleiades, the enchanted call of a nightingale, the heady crunch of blanched asparagus. He traveled far more than most of his generation: Germany, Holland, Denmark, Norway, Sweden, England, France, Spain, Switzerland, Italy, Bulgaria, Hungary, Romania, Czechoslovakia, Libya, Morocco, the United States, Cuba, Mexico.

What distinguished Dietrich most was his sensitive blending of the world of religion and the world of reason. Although his mother and governesses were pietists, his father and brothers were agnostics, given more to the evidence of science than to the hopes of Christianity. In a half dozen books, Dietrich struggled with the questions that always had gnawed at him. How real is God? Does God really care? Why does God allow suffering? What is the role of the church? For himself at least, Dietrich finally found convincing answers after a long and painful quest. Man is God's instrument on earth, made in His image, responsible, redeemed in Christ, enlightened by God's Spirit, and self-fulfilling.

As a thinker and writer, Dietrich expressed his ideas most clearly and delightfully in two books, *The Cost of Discipleship* and *Letters and Papers from Prison*. The first is theoretical and the second practical. Both were published posthumously. The young Dietrich, who began life as an aesthete and an aristocrat, when confined behind steel bars became far more human and realistic. For himself and for his contemporaries, Dietrich tried to make the world grow up, to "come of age." He contemplated, he struggled, he matured. Those who read him now can better understand their own searchings and conflicts because he experienced them first.

Selected Bibliography

Bailey, J. Martin. *Steps of Bonhoeffer: A Pictorial Album.* Philadelphia: United Church Press, 1969.

Bethge, Eberhard. *Dietrich Bonhoeffer: Man of Vision.* New York: Harper and Row, 1970.

Bonhoeffer, Dietrich. *Gesammelte Schriften.* 4 vols. Munich: Christian Kaiser, 1958–61.

———. *Letters and Papers from Prison.* Translated by Reginald Fuller. New York: Macmillan, 1967.

———. *The Way to Freedom.* Translated by John Bowden. New York: Harper and Row, 1966.

Bosanquet, Mary. *Life and Death of Dietrich Bonhoeffer.* New York: Harper and Row, 1969.

Dumas, Andre. *Dietrich Bonhoeffer: Theologian of Reality.* Translated by Robert M. Brown. New York: Macmillan, 1971.

Gill, Theodore A. *Dietrich Bonhoeffer: Memo for a Movie.* New York: Macmillan, 1970.

Leibholz-Bonhoeffer, Sabine. *The Bonhoeffers: Portrait of a Family.* London: Sidgwick & Jackson, 1968.

Marty, Martin E. *The Place of Bonhoeffer: Problems and Possibilities in His Thought.* Greenwood, 1981.

Mehta, Ved. *New Theologian.* New York: Harper and Row, 1966.

Ott, Heinrich. *Reality and Faith: The Theological Legacy of Dietrich Bonhoeffer.* Philadelphia: Fortress, 1972.

Wind, Renate. *Dietrich Bonhoeffer: A Spoke in the Wheel.* Grand Rapids: Eerdmans, 1992.

Woelfel, James W. *Bonhoeffer's Theology: Classical and Revolutionary.* Nashville: Abingdon, 1970.

Zimmermann, Wolf-Dieter et al. *I Knew Dietrich Bonhoeffer.* Translated by Kaethe Gregor Smith. New York: Harper and Row, 1966.